W9-BUQ-993

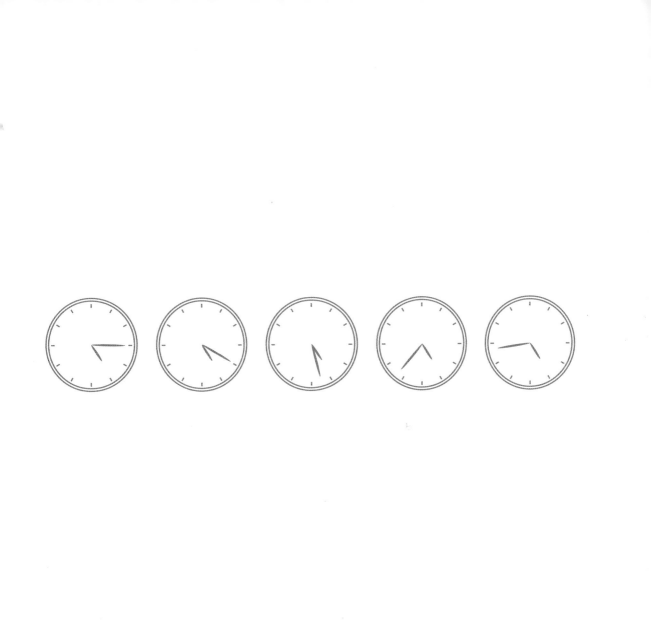

THE
pressure
cooker
COOKBOOK

RECIPES Tori Ritchie

PHOTOGRAPHS Sheri Giblin

weldon**owen**

contents

pressure cookers for today

Everyone seems to be looking for a new way to save time in the kitchen, but the solution has been there all along: pressure cookers. These ingenious devices, originally marketed in the early 1900s, were designed to speed up cooking by using a simple principle: seal the lid to create pressure, which causes the temperature in the pot to rise past boiling, and food cooks faster. No invisible microwaves, no food-altering science, just simple, clean steam.

Fast-forward to today and pressure cookers have many compelling reasons for their renewed popularity. Many dishes that are too often relegated to Sunday dinner or ordered in restaurants because they take too long to prepare at home—pot roast, short ribs, baked beans—can be prepared in one-half to two-thirds the time it takes to cook them conventionally. You don't even have to plan ahead. But pressure cookers also help the home cook save money. The foods cooked in a pressure cooker are generally tougher and less desirable than more tender foods, and thus less expensive. Finally, pressure cookers keep in foods' nutrients. While these cooking vessels allow you to make comforting meals on a weeknight schedule, pressure cookers are also a perfect addition to a healthy lifestyle (see right).

Pressure cookers aren't limited to just soups, stews, and sauces. Using the recipes in these pages, you'll learn how to make a shortcut risotto as good as the original in just six minutes, or butternut squash purée, orange-scented beets, braised artichokes, chicken thighs, and even corned beef—all in a flash. Flavors vary widely from the chiles of Mexico, to the soy glazes of Asia, to the creamy sauces of France.

A HEALTHIER WAY TO COOK

Because everything cooks faster in a pressure cooker, and only a small amount of liquid is needed, fewer nutrients are leached or evaporated away as they are in other types of cooking. Some people have a cooker on hand just to make high-fiber, protein-rich beans weekly or even daily, or to cook whole-grain brown rice or farro at the last minute, both of which contribute to a healthy lifestyle.

ABOUT OLDER
PRESSURE COOKERS

If you already own a pressure cooker that was made in the last decade or so, it may be fine to use, but you will need to check that the gasket or sealing ring is not dried, cracked, or worn out; that you have all the parts in good working order; and that you have the instruction manual. If you are missing anything or have doubts, contact the manufacturer. Your best bet may be to invest in a new one.

modern pressure cooking

The pressure cooker isn't a new tool, but it is a completely redesigned one. The original models were variations on large, pressurized canning kettles that became popular around the time of the first World War. Manufacturers saw the potential to adapt these for home cooking. Soon, the pressure cooker was the appliance of the moment and vendors across the country rushed inexpensive versions to market to meet demand.

When World War II came along, most manufacturers retooled their factories to help the war effort. Pressure cookers were put on the back burner, so to speak, and new pots weren't introduced. Older pots stayed in use too long, which is why some people have bad memories of them. These were the ones with ominous jiggling valves and sinister hissing steam—the ones Mom struggled with to unscrew the lid. Worse yet, stories circulated about being scalded or tomato sauce on the kitchen ceiling when the top blew. Then there was the food: uniformly bland, overcooked, and pallid. Needless to say, pressure cookers faded out of fashion in America. In Europe however, cooks continued to use the pots to prepare traditional slow-cooked dishes in much less time, and manufacturers there continued to update the models and make them better. There, the technology evolved, as did the quality of recipes associated with pressure cooking.

Back in the US, demand for cooking shortcuts never faded, so smart manufacturers revisited pressure cookers in the 1980s, employing improved technology to eliminate mishaps. Today's pressure cookers have built-in safety features, including secure pressure-regulator valves and at least three backup systems to release steam in the event of a blockage. A modern stove-top pressure cooker simply cannot be opened while still cooking under pressure.

Once these new-and-improved pressure cookers came to market and received rave reviews, demand went up. As a result, there was a boom in cookbooks and food articles with intriguing recipes to make in the pots: think beer-braised chicken, beef stroganoff, and scalloped potatoes. Recipes from overseas migrated here, too: Bolognese sauce, braised fennel, and even risotto. Gradually, cooks everywhere adapted their own recipes to pressure cooking so that now there are countless Web sites dedicated to the appliance and its many uses and fans. Recently, electric pressure cookers have been introduced, adding increased safety, convenience, and ease for the home cook.

As mentioned before, part of the pressure cooker's popularity is the increased awareness today of health and whole foods. There's an environmentally friendly aspect to cooking under pressure, too. Because it takes far less time to cook a dish, less gas or electricity is used. And saving energy is good for everyone.

WHAT SIZE POT?

Pressure cookers today come in a range of sizes, but for the average household, a six-quart pressure cooker is the most convenient, multi-purpose size.

WHY USE A PRESSURE COOKER?

- Contemporary models are safe and reliable

- Less cooking time means more energy saved

- Healthy foods, such as whole grains, beans, and legumes, cook quickly, while retaining more nutrients

- Comfort foods can be prepared on a weeknight schedule

- Vegetables, potatoes, and even risotto need no tending when cooked under pressure

- Dishes cook in one third to one half the time

average pressure cook times

FOOD	COOKING TIME	LEVEL	RELEASE METHOD
Black Beans	25 minutes	high	natural steam release
Chickpeas, dried	40 minutes	high	natural steam release
Lentils	8 minutes	high	natural steam release
Navy Beans, dried	25 minutes	high	natural steam release
Pinto Beans, dried	18–20 minutes	high	natural steam release
Barley	15–18 minutes	high	natural steam release
Risotto	6 minutes	high	quick steam release
Wild Rice	25 minutes	high	quick steam release
Chicken Breast	7–10 minutes	high	natural steam release
Chicken Thighs	8–12 minutes	high	natural steam release
Chicken, Whole	10 minutes	high	quick steam release
Turkey Breast	30 minutes	high	natural steam release
Bone-in Pork Shoulder	40–50 minutes	high	natural steam release
Boneless Pork Shoulder	15 minutes	high	natural steam release
Boneless Lamb Meat	15 minutes	high	natural steam release
Beef Brisket	50–60 minutes	high	quick steam release
Beef Round	18–20 minutes	high	quick steam release
Artichokes, quartered	4 minutes	high	quick steam release
Beets	20 minutes	high	quick steam release
Butternut squash, cut into 2-inch (5 cm) cubes	8 minutes	high	quick steam release
Cauliflower florets	2 minutes	high	quick steam release
Mustard Greens, 1-inch (2.5 cm) strips	6 minutes	high	quick steam release
Pearl Onions	3 minutes	high	quick steam release
Potatoes, ¼ inch (6 mm) chunks	4 minutes	high	quick steam release
Red cabbage, cut into thin strips	5 minutes	high	quick steam release

the right pressure cooker for you

With the various types of pressure cookers on the market today, both stove top and electric models, cooking under pressure is just a shopping trip away. Your decision on which model to choose will probably be based on three factors: which size pot suits your household; price; and the amount of storage space in your kitchen. Both types of pressure cookers have advantages and either is a good choice. It's a matter of individual taste and preference.

Stove-top pressure cookers Stove-top models are generally available in aluminum or stainless steel, the former being more inexpensive and lightweight, the latter being of a heavier gauge and costing slightly more. While the choice is individual, the recommendation is the same as with all pots and pans: a heavy, durable metal with a sturdy base will distribute heat evenly, yield good results, and last for a long time. Stainless steel pots provide all these qualities. Plus, they often have the advantage over aluminum pots of being dishwasher safe.

Electric pressure cookers Electric models offer unique features. They don't take up space on the stove top, which leaves your range free for other purposes. They have built-in timers that are very precise, eliminating the margin of error in cooking times. Electric pressure cookers also ensure consistent heat; with a stove top model, you need to adjust the gas or electric burner to maintain the cooking pressure at the optimum level, while an electric cooker does this automatically (see *Adjusting Pressure*, page 15). In short, you can walk away from an electric model while it cooks, but it is better to keep an occasional eye on a stove top model. The downsides to owning an electric pressure cooker include storage constraints (not everyone has space on his or her counter or in the cupboard for another appliance) and that these models generally cost more than stove top pressure cookers.

ABOUT THE RECIPES

The recipes in this book were developed for a six-quart pot, which is the perfect size for family meals of four to six servings, plus the occasional recipe for larger crowds or when you want leftovers, such as with soups, stews, beans, or brisket.

WHAT IS PSI?

The pressure built up under the lid is measured as PSI, or pounds per square inch. High pressure in most cookers is 13 to 15 PSI and 250°F (38 degrees above boiling point at sea level) and is the setting used for most recipes. Low pressure (available on some models) is used primarily for steaming.

how the pressure cooker works

Every pressure cooker, whether stove top or electric, is made up of four basic parts: a cooking pot, a lid, a sealing ring or gasket, and valves. In order to understand how they all work, the first step is to read the instruction manual cover to cover. Even if you never read manuals, you must do so in this case. Every pressure cooker model is slightly different and this is the only way to learn how to use yours.

The pot As mentioned before, stove top pressure cookers are made of either aluminum or stainless steel, while electric models are usually a combination of metal and plastic (for the exterior casing and dials). Many stainless steel pots have a base with three-ply construction layered with either an aluminum or copper core. This helps conduct heat evenly, which is a plus when browning or sautéing foods in the pot prior to pressure cooking (an essential step in developing flavor in many recipes). Some electric pots have a nonstick interior surface, which makes for scorchless browning and easy cleaning.

The lid The pressure cooker lid locks onto the pot, creating a secure seal. For both stove top and electric pressure cookers, this is usually done by aligning the handles. Most lids will click audibly when put into place properly. Once the lid is locked and the pressure level is selected, steam will build up, creating pressure (see *What is PSI?* left), and an indicator tells you when pressure has been reached.

The gasket The lid of a pressure cooker is lined with a flexible (usually rubber) sealing ring, or gasket, that creates an airtight seal. The gasket must be cleaned and maintained after every use; the instruction manual will indicate the best way to do this. The gasket must also be inspected before every use to make sure it has not dried out, cracked, or stiffened. Most manufacturers recommend that you replace the gasket every year if you use your pressure cooker regularly.

The valves The lid is also where you find the pressure-regulator valve (sometimes called "pressure-limit valve"). The valve takes various forms, depending on the style of pressure cooker you buy. If it is detachable, it is paramount that you do not lose it because the pot cannot function without a pressure-regluator valve. There is a minimum of three other built-in valves on a modern pressure cooker, which may or may not be as obvious to you as the pressure-regulator valve. These are designed to be safety devices and will relieve excess pressure in the event of a malfunction.

Depending on the recipe, the pressure has to be released after cooking either naturally by letting the steam release on its own (during which time the food continues to cook), or by quick-releasing the steam (see *Releasing Pressure* on page 17), in which the cooking stops relatively quickly. Once the pressure-regulator valve indicates that the pressure is reduced to zero, the lid can be opened.

Other features and tools Electric pressure cookers have built-in timers and other convenient functions, such as sautéing, browning, and simmering, built into the pot. When using a stove-top model, you will need a reliable digital timer to count down the minutes the food cooks once pressure is reached. Otherwise, no special tools are required for your pressure cooker. Some models come with a steamer insert or rack; consult the manual for when to use those.

While it seems like a lot of parts compared to a conventional pot, the logic becomes very clear the first time you cook in your pressure cooker: Put in the food, browning or sautéing it first as necessary; add the liquid; lock the lid into place; select the level of pressure desired; turn on the heat; and set the timer. It won't be long before a succulent stew, a bowl of creamy beans, a tender roast, or a rich mound of scalloped potatoes is on the table.

ADJUSTING PRESSURE

With a stove top model, once pressure is reached you'll need to adjust the burner beneath the pot so that a steady trickle of steam emits from the valve. If you have a high heat, commercial-style range, you may need to use a diffuser pad to maintain proper pressure, even on the lowest setting. On an electric range, preheat a second burner to a lower temperature and move the pot to that burner to quickly adjust pressure. If you have an electric pressure cooker, it will automatically adjust the heat to maintain optimum pressure.

basic steps to success under pressure

So many foods are superb when cooked under pressure that it may be hard to choose where to begin when you open this book. Whatever you choose, these steps will ensure success.

preparing ingredients The size of the food pieces needs to be uniform so that everything cooks at the same pace, so follow the instructions in the recipe on how to cut ingredients such as meat, potatoes, carrots, celery, and onions.

browning Many foods, especially meats and poultry, benefit from browning first to develop flavor, so it's important to know how to do this: Heat the fat (oil or butter or both) until it shimmers before adding food. Don't crowd the pot; add just enough pieces to cover the bottom with a few spaces in between; you should hear a good deal of sizzling. Turn the food only when it pulls away easily from the bottom, using tongs; don't yank it. When browning in a stove top model, be sure not to turn the heat up so high that flames lick the sides of the pot or you could melt the handles. If the bottom of the pot starts to scorch, add a little water to lower the heat and release the brown bits.

adding liquid As none of the cooking liquid will evaporate during pressure cooking, most recipes call for a minimum amount of liquid to be added to the pot. Check the instruction manual for your model to find out what is required.

using seasonings Add tender fresh herbs, such as mint and basil, at the end of cooking or the flavors will dissipate. Hardier herbs, such as thyme or rosemary, stand up well to the heat and can be added at the start. Dry herbs need to be added in greater amounts than you'd use in conventional recipes because flavors are concentrated.

salting When you first combine the ingredients, salt them lightly to bring out the flavors (even with beans, despite what you may have read elsewhere), then adjust the salt to taste just before serving.

working with foaming foods Rice, beans, and a few other ingredients foam up in a pressure cooker and can clog valves. To prevent this, drizzle a tablespoon of olive oil or canola oil over the cooking liquid just before you close the pot; don't stir. Buy beans in bulk from a store with high turnover to ensure a good result.

releasing pressure Depending on the type of food, once cooking is completed, pressure is released either naturally, by letting the pot stand, or by quick-releasing the steam out of the pressure-regulator valve (See *Releasing Pressure*, right). Bear in mind that the natural-release method can take from a few minutes to half an hour, depending on the volume of food in the pot, so be sure to account for this in your serving plans.

opening the pot Even after pressure is released, there is still steam under the lid and it is HOT. When you open the pressure cooker, always tilt the lid away from your face to avoid getting scalded.

thickening sauces Because there is less evaporation in a sealed pressure cooker, some sauces for stews and other dishes may need to be thickened at the end of cooking. In most cases, it's best to reduce the sauce in the pot, uncovered, rather than adding a thickener, such as cornstarch. Or, strain the sauce into a frying pan and reduce it even more quickly on the stove top.

cooling down Ingredients are extremely hot when they come out of a pressure cooker, so let the food stand for about five minutes to cool down and settle the flavors before serving.

RELEASING PRESSURE

To release pressure naturally, turn off the heat (an electric model will do this automatically) and let the pot stand until the indicator shows that pressure has completely dissipated.

To quick-release pressure, follow the instructions in the manual: it will usually be by opening the pressure-release valve while the pot is still on the stove top. When doing this, turn on your kitchen ventilation and use a long-handled wooden spoon or tongs to adjust the valve in order to keep your hands away from the steam.

Some older pressure cooker models call for placing the pot under running cold water in the sink, but this method can be tricky.

soups & stews

PRESSURE COOK TIME

9 minutes

QUICK STEAM RELEASE

A Moroccan spice mix called *ras al hanout* traditionally gives this soup extra warmth. Here, you can blend your own for a rich vegetarian soup that is ready in only 9 minutes instead of the usual half hour. Arborio rice works well in this recipe.

moroccan-style tomato-rice soup

small yellow onion, 1, finely chopped

olive oil, 3 tbsp

ground cumin, ground ginger, and ground coriander, 1½ tsp *each*

paprika, 1½ tsp

salt

cayenne pepper, ¼ tsp

ripe red tomatoes, 2 lb (1 kg), peeled, seeded, and crushed (about 3 cups)

low-sodium vegetable broth, 4 cups (32 fl oz/1 l)

tomato paste, ¼ cup (2 oz/60 g)

sugar, 1 tbsp

short-grain white rice, ⅓ cup (2½ oz/75 g)

bay leaf, 1

chopped fresh cilantro for garnish

MAKES 4 SERVINGS

In the pressure cooker pot, sauté the onion in the oil until golden, about 3 minutes. Stir in the cumin, ginger, coriander, paprika, ½ teaspoon salt, and the cayenne. Cook for 30 seconds. Stir in the tomatoes, then add the broth, tomato paste, and sugar and stir until blended. Add the rice and bay leaf. If using an electric pressure cooker, switch off the sauté function.

Lock the lid into place and cook on high pressure for 9 minutes. Quick-release the steam (see page 17). When the pressure valve drops, remove the lid, tilting it away from your face to allow residual steam to escape. Let the soup stand for 5 minutes to cool down, then discard the bay leaf. Ladle into bowls, garnish with cilantro, and serve right away.

This soup usually takes almost an hour to cook. Here is a light version of the classic recipe made with beef meatballs so it's both fast to cook and fun to eat. You can substitute farro for the barley, if you like; the two grains are very similar.

easy beef & barley soup

ground chuck, ¾ lb
(375 g)

Worcestershire sauce,
1 tbsp

**salt and freshly ground
pepper**

fresh flat-leaf parsley,
¼ cup (⅓ oz/10 g) minced

parmesan cheese, ¼ cup
(1 oz/30 g) grated

large egg, 1, beaten

garlic, 1 clove, pressed

yellow onion, 1, chopped

carrots, 2, chopped

butter, 2 tbsp

olive oil, 1 tbsp

chopped tomatoes,
1 can (14 oz/440 g)

pearl barley, 1 cup
(6 oz/185 g)

**low-sodium chicken broth
and beef broth,** 3 cups
(24 fl oz/750 ml) *each*

MAKES 6–8 SERVINGS

To make the meatballs, put the meat in a bowl and sprinkle it with the Worcestershire sauce, ½ teaspoon salt, and ½ teaspoon pepper. Add the parsley, cheese, egg, and garlic and blend the mixture with your hands. Shape into small meatballs about 1 inch (2.5 cm) in diameter. Set aside.

In the pressure cooker pot, sauté the onion and carrots in the butter and oil until softened, about 5 minutes. Add the tomatoes and stir well. Rinse the barley in a small sieve, then stir it into the vegetables. Add the chicken and beef broths and meatballs to the pot. If using an electric pressure cooker, switch off the sauté function.

Lock the lid into place and cook on high pressure for 8 minutes. Let the steam release naturally (see page 17). When the pressure valve drops, remove the lid, tilting it away from your face to allow residual steam to escape. Let the soup stand for 5 minutes to settle the flavors and cool down. Serve right away.

This classic duo of potatoes and leeks can be served cold, as vichyssoise, or sipped warm. The mild base cooks for a fraction of the usual 30 minutes. Add enrichments such as cooked ham and garnish with chives after puréeing to make the flavors pop.

potato-leek soup two ways

leeks, 2 lb (1 kg)

russet potatoes, 1½ lb (750 g)

butter, 2 tbsp

salt

low-sodium chicken broth, 5 cups (40 fl oz/ 1.25 l)

chives, snipped

for the hot soup

half-and-half, 1½ cups (12 fl oz/375 ml)

frozen corn kernels, 1 cup (6 oz/185 g), thawed

cooked ham, chopped, 1 cup (6 oz/185 g)

for the cold soup

cucumber, 1

half-and-half, 1 cup (8 fl oz/250 ml)

sour cream, 1 cup (8 oz/250 g)

MAKES 6–8 SERVINGS

Cut the roots and green tops off the leeks. Slice the white parts of the leeks in half lengthwise, then thinly slice crosswise. Put the sliced leeks in a bowl of cold water and swish vigorously to rinse them of grit. Lift out the rinsed leeks with a sieve and set aside. Discard the water. Peel the potatoes and cut them into 1-inch (2.5-cm) cubes.

In the pressure cooker pot, sauté the leeks in the butter until soft, about 4 minutes. Sprinkle lightly with salt, then add the broth and the potatoes. If using an electric pressure cooker, switch off the sauté function.

Lock the lid into place and cook on high pressure for 4 minutes. Quick-release the steam (see page 17). When the pressure valve drops, remove the lid, tilting it away from your face to allow residual steam to escape. Let the soup stand until it has slightly cooled and is no longer steaming, then purée it in batches in a blender (or with an immersion blender directly in the pot) until smooth.

To serve the soup hot, pour the puréed soup into a clean saucepan. Add the half-and-half and corn and cook over medium heat, stirring often, until hot, about 5 minutes. Stir in the ham. If you like a thinner soup, add more broth. Season with salt, ladle into bowls, and sprinkle with the chives.

To serve the soup cold, cool the puréed soup to room temperature, transfer it to a large container and refrigerate, covered, until chilled. Meanwhile, peel, seed, and finely dice the cucumber; set aside. Whisk in the half-and-half and sour cream until smooth. If you like a thinner soup, add more broth. Stir in the cucumber, season with salt, and ladle into bowls. Sprinkle with the chives.

This soup is deceptive: it's smooth and creamy, but contains no dairy products. Instead, a potato added to the base gives the soup silkiness. Its hearty flavor will also deceive, since it takes only 5 minutes instead of the usual 25.

curried cauliflower soup with spicy croutons

white potato, 1, about 6 oz (185 g)

cauliflower, 1 head

small yellow onion, 1, chopped

butter, 1 tbsp

low-sodium vegetable or chicken broth, 5 cups (40 fl oz/1.25 l)

salt

Madras curry powder, 1½ tsp

Spicy Croutons (page 98) for garnish

MAKES 6 SERVINGS

Peel the potato and cut it into 1-inch (2.5-cm) pieces. Remove any leaves from the cauliflower and cut out the core; chop the remaining cauliflower into 1-inch (2.5-cm) pieces.

In the pressure cooker pot, sauté the onion in the butter until softened, about 2 minutes. Add the broth, potato, cauliflower, and ½ teaspoon salt. If using an electric pressure cooker, switch off the sauté function.

Lock the lid into place and cook on high pressure for 5 minutes. Quick-release the steam (see page 17). When the pressure valve drops, remove the lid, tilting it away from your face to allow residual steam to escape.

Stir the curry powder into the soup. Let the soup stand until no longer steaming hot, then purée it in batches in a blender (or with an immersion blender directly in the pot) until very smooth. Return the puréed soup to the pot and season to taste with salt; reheat if necessary. Ladle into bowls, top with the croutons, and serve right away.

Farro is a unique strain of wheat, also called *emmer wheat*, which has been eaten in Italy since Roman times; it can now be found in many grocery stores. Look for semi-pearled *(semiperlato)* farro, which helps to cut down the cooking time by 80 percent.

tuscan farro & lentil soup

semi-pearled farro,
¾ cup (2 oz/60 g)

dried brown or green lentils, 1½ cups
(10 oz/315 g)

yellow onion, 1, chopped

celery, 2 stalks, diced
½-inch (12-mm)

large carrots, 2, diced

olive oil, 3 tbsp

garlic, 2 cloves, minced

fresh rosemary, 1½ tsp
minced

low-sodium vegetable or chicken broth, 4 cups
(32 fl oz/1 l)

baby spinach or arugula leaves, 6 cups loosely
packed (6 oz/185 g)

salt and freshly ground pepper

MAKES 8 SERVINGS

Put the farro in a small sieve, rinse under cold water, shake the sieve to get rid of excess water, then pour the farro into a bowl. Rinse and shake the lentils in the same way and add them to the farro; set the bowl aside.

In the pressure cooker pot, sauté the onion, celery, and carrots in 2 tablespoons of the oil until softened, about 5 minutes. Stir in the garlic and rosemary and cook for 30 seconds. Add the farro and lentils and pour in the broth and 4 cups (32 fl oz/1 l) water. Drizzle the remaining 1 tablespoon oil over the liquid; do not stir. If using an electric pressure cooker, switch off the sauté function.

Lock the lid into place and cook on high pressure for 8 minutes. Let the steam release naturally (see page 17). When the pressure valve drops, remove the lid, tilting it away from your face to allow residual steam to escape. Stir in the spinach until wilted, then let the soup stand for 5 minutes to cool down. Season the soup to taste with salt and pepper and serve right away.

The smokiness in this delicious recipe comes from Spanish *pimentón*, or smoked sweet paprika. Thawed frozen green peas are whirled in at the end, to make a brightly colored soup that takes one-fourth of the usual cooking time.

smoky split pea soup

yellow onion, 1, chopped

celery, 2 stalks, finely diced

carrots, 2, finely diced

olive oil, 3 tbsp, plus additional for drizzling

smoked sweet paprika (*pimentón*), 2 tsp, plus additional for sprinkling

salt

dried split peas, 1 lb (500 g), rinsed and picked over

low-sodium vegetable or chicken broth, 8 cups (64 fl oz/2 l)

bay leaf, 1

frozen peas, 2 cups (10 oz/315 g), thawed

freshly ground pepper

MAKES 8 SERVINGS

In the pressure cooker pot, sauté the onion, celery, and carrots in 2 tablespoons of the oil until softened, about 5 minutes. Stir in the paprika and ½ teaspoon salt and cook for 30 seconds. Add the split peas, broth, and bay leaf, pushing the bay leaf below the surface with a spoon. Drizzle the remaining 1 tablespoon oil over the liquid, but do not stir. If using an electric pressure cooker, switch off the sauté function.

Lock the lid into place and cook on high pressure for 10 minutes. Let the steam release naturally (see page 17). When the pressure valve drops, remove the lid, tilting it away from your face to allow residual steam to escape. Discard the bay leaf. With a measuring cup or ladle, scoop 1 cup (8 fl oz/250 ml) of the soup from the pot and put it in a blender; add the thawed peas and 1 cup (8 fl oz/250 ml) water and blend until puréed.

Stir the purée back into the soup, then season to taste with salt and pepper. Ladle the soup into bowls and drizzle each portion with olive oil and sprinkle with a pinch of smoked paprika. Serve right away (the bright green color of the peas will fade as the soup stands).

Texas-style chili has no beans. It's traditionally a long-simmered dish made with beef stew meat (such as chuck) and an assortment of chile peppers and spices. For the most authentic taste, use pure ground chiles, rather than blended chili powder.

texas-style chili

beef chuck, 3 lb (1.5 kg), cut into 1-inch (2.5-cm) cubes

salt

canola oil, 3 tbsp

yellow onion, 1, chopped

garlic, 2 cloves, minced

ground ancho chile, 3 tbsp

sweet paprika, 1 tbsp

ground cumin, 2 tsp

dried oregano leaves, 1 tsp

tomato paste, 1/2 cup (4 oz/125 g)

for the optional garnishes

sour cream, 1 cup (8 oz/250 g)

Cheddar cheese, 1 cup grated (4 oz/125 g)

green onions, 4, sliced

MAKES 4–6 SERVINGS

Pat the meat dry with paper towels and season it lightly all over with salt. In the pressure cooker pot, brown the meat in 2 tablespoons of the oil in batches, turning with tongs as necessary; transfer each batch to a plate as it is cooked. After removing the last batch, add the onion and the remaining 1 tablespoon oil and cook until softened. Stir in the garlic and cook for 30 seconds. Stir in the chile, paprika, cumin, and oregano. Pour in 1½ cups (12 fl oz/375 ml) water, then stir in the tomato paste until blended. Return the meat and any accumulated juices to the pot; stir to coat the meat with sauce. If using an electric pressure cooker, switch off the sauté function.

Lock the lid into place and cook on high pressure for 15 minutes. Let the steam release naturally (see page 17). When the pressure valve drops, remove the lid, tilting it away from your face to allow residual steam to escape. Let the chili stand for 5 minutes to settle the flavors. Ladle into bowls and top each portion with sour cream, cheese, and green onions, as desired. Serve right away.

Like traditional chile verde, this simple stew contains lots of roasted green chiles. However, it doesn't take the typical 1½ hours to cook and has a surprise addition: hominy. For a greener stew, stir in 2 cups (2 oz/60 g) of baby spinach before serving.

pork chile verde

New Mexico or Anaheim chiles, 1 lb (500 g), roasted, peeled, and seeded; or two 7-oz (220-g) cans roasted whole green chiles

boneless pork shoulder, 2½ lb (1.25 kg), cut into 1-inch (2.5-cm) cubes

salt

canola oil, 3 tbsp

white onion, 1, chopped

fresh cilantro leaves, 1 cup (1 oz/30 g) packed, minced, plus sprigs for garnish

garlic, 2 cloves, minced

dried oregano leaves, 1 tbsp

low-sodium chicken broth, 2 cups (16 fl oz/500 ml)

yellow hominy, 1 can (15 oz/470 g), drained

lime, 1, cut into wedges

MAKES 4–6 SERVINGS

Slice the fresh chiles crosswise into thin strips (if using canned chiles, drain them first, then slit open 1 side so that they lay flat; slice into strips). Set the chile strips aside.

Pat the pork dry with paper towels and season lightly all over with salt. In the pressure cooker pot, brown the pork in 2 tablespoons of the oil in batches, turning with tongs as necessary; transfer each batch to a plate as it is cooked. After removing the last batch, add the onion and the remaining 1 tablespoon oil to the pot and cook until softened. Stir in the minced cilantro, garlic, and oregano and cook for 30 seconds. Add the chiles and cook for 1 minute more. Return the browned pork and any accumulated juices to the pot and pour in the broth. If using an electric pressure cooker, switch off the browning function.

Lock the lid into place and cook on high pressure for 15 minutes. Let the steam release naturally (see page 17). When the pressure valve drops, remove the lid, tilting it away from your face to allow residual steam to escape. Stir in the hominy, then let the stew stand for 10 minutes to heat the hominy through. To serve, ladle into a large serving bowl or individual bowls and garnish with lime wedges and cilantro sprigs.

Black beans can take 2 hours to cook, which is why pressure cooking makes such sense for them. A little bit of salt helps the beans hold their shape. For vegetarian chili, substitute 8 ounces sliced mushrooms and some diced green chiles for the sausages.

black bean chili

yellow onion, 1, chopped

large red bell pepper, 1, diced

canola oil, 3 tbsp

chicken habañero sausages (fully cooked), 12 oz (375 g)

chili powder, 2 tbsp

dried oregano, 1 tsp

diced tomatoes, 1 can (14½ oz/455 g)

frozen corn kernels, ½ cup (3 oz/90 g), thawed

cooked black beans (page 98)

for the garnishes

sour cream, 1 cup (8 oz/250 g)

jack cheese, 1 cup shredded (4 oz/125 g)

fresh cilantro, ¼ cup chopped (⅓ oz/10 g)

MAKES 4 SERVINGS

In the pressure cooker pot, sauté the onion and bell pepper in 2 tablespoons of the oil until softened, about 5 minutes. Slice the sausages into pieces that are ¼ inch (6 mm) thick and add them to the pot. Cook, stirring, until the sausages sizzle and take on a little color, about 2 minutes. Stir in the chili powder and oregano, then add 1½ cups (12 fl oz/375 ml) water, the tomatoes, corn, and beans. Pour the remaining 1 tablespoon oil over the top, but do not stir. If using an electric pressure cooker, switch off the sauté function.

Lock the lid into place and cook on high pressure for 5 minutes. Quick-release the steam (see page 17). When the pressure valve drops, remove the lid, tilting it away from your face to allow residual steam to escape. Stir the chili, then let it stand for 5 minutes. Ladle into bowls and garnish with the sour cream, cheese, and cilantro, as desired. Serve right away.

Traditional Irish stew gets a spring-green update with leeks, herbs, and peas. It usually takes 90 minutes for the meat to become tender and flavorful, but the pressure cooker does it in a jiffy. You can substitute bone-in lamb for even more flavor.

springtime irish stew

boneless lamb stew (shoulder) meat, 3 lb (1.5 kg), cut into 2-inch (5-cm) chunks

salt and freshly ground pepper

canola oil, 2 tbsp

butter, 1 tbsp

leeks, 2, cleaned, roots and green tops removed, sliced

Boquet Garni (page 98)

low-sodium beef or chicken broth, 2 cups (16 fl oz/500 ml), plus extra if needed

small red potatoes (creamers), 1 lb (500 g)

large carrots, 4

frozen peas, 1 cup (5 oz/155 g), thawed

apple cider vinegar, 2 tbsp

dried dill weed, 2 tsp

MAKES 6 SERVINGS

Pat the meat dry with paper towels and season lightly all over with salt and pepper. In the pressure cooker pot, brown the meat in the oil in batches, turning with tongs; transfer each batch to a plate as it is cooked.

After removing the last batch of meat from the pot, add the butter and leeks and cook until softened, about 3 minutes. Add the bouquet garni and broth, then return the browned meat and juices to the pot. If using an electric pressure cooker, switch off the browning function.

Lock the lid into place and cook on high pressure for 15 minutes. Let the steam release naturally (see page 17). When the pressure valve drops, remove the lid, tilting it away from your face to allow residual steam to escape. Meanwhile, cut the potatoes into quarters. Peel the carrots and cut them into chunks about 2 inches (5 cm) long and 1 inch (2.5 cm) thick.

After removing the lid, lift out the meat and mound it in the center of a large platter; cover with foil. Discard the bouquet garni. Put the potatoes in the pot; scatter the carrots on top and sprinkle lightly with salt, but do not stir. Lock the lid into place and cook on high pressure for 5 minutes, then quick-release the steam (see page 17). When the pressure valve drops, remove the lid, tilting it away from your face to allow residual steam to escape.

With a slotted spoon, divide the potatoes, carrots, and meat among individual bowls. Stir the peas, vinegar, and dill into the pot, turn on the heat (or use the simmer function on an electric cooker) and simmer until the peas are heated through, about 2 minutes. Spoon the sauce and peas over the meat and vegetables in the bowls and serve right away.

beans & grains

Like most beans, chickpeas can take 2 hours to cook. Here, they quickly emerge with a meaty texture and flavor that's more satisfying than canned. Serve with grilled lamb, chicken, or fish, or alone as a vegetarian entrée.

chickpeas with lemon, oregano & olives

dried chickpeas,
1½ cups (9 oz/280 g)

garlic, 4 cloves, peeled

bay leaf, 1

salt

olive oil, 5 tbsp
(3 fl oz/80 ml)

**fresh flat-leaf parsley
leaves,** 1½ cups packed
(1½ oz/45 g)

fresh oregano leaves,
2 tbsp chopped

fresh lemon zest, 1 tbsp
coarsely grated

**freshly squeezed lemon
juice,** about 2 tbsp

**pitted good-quality
green olives,** ½ cup
(2½ oz/75 g), roughly
chopped

MAKES 6 SERVINGS

Rinse the chickpeas in a sieve under cold water. Pick over and remove any stones or misshapen chickpeas. In the pressure cooker pot, combine the chickpeas, 6 cups (48 fl oz/1.5 l) water, 2 of the garlic cloves, the bay leaf, and ½ teaspoon salt. Drizzle 1 tablespoon of the oil over the liquid.

Lock the lid into place and cook on high pressure for 40 minutes. Let the steam release naturally (see page 17). When the pressure valve drops, remove the lid, tilting it away from your face to allow residual steam to escape. Test a chickpea for doneness: it should be cooked through, but not soft. If it is too firm, lock the lid into place again and cook on high pressure for 5 minutes more; quick-release the steam (see page 17).

Drain the chickpeas in a colander, reserving the cooking liquid. Discard the bay leaf. Clean and dry the pressure cooker pot. (At this point, the chickpeas and liquid can be cooled, covered, and refrigerated separately for up to 1 day. To continue, let them come to room temperature before proceeding with the recipe.)

On a cutting board, mince together the parsley, oregano, remaining 2 garlic cloves, and lemon zest. In the pressure cooker pot (or a sauté pan on the stove, if chickpeas were made ahead), sauté the herb-garlic mixture in the remaining 4 tablespoons (2 fl oz/60 ml) oil until fragrant, about 1 minute. Add the cooked chickpeas, lemon juice, 1 cup (8 fl oz/250 ml) reserved cooking liquid, and the olives; stir for a few minutes until the flavors are blended, adding more cooking liquid if the mixture seems dry. Season to taste with salt and more lemon juice to taste, then serve.

Even though using the pressure cooker negates the need to cook these for 2 hours, these beans still have that distinctive smoky-sweet flavor that comes from long cooking. Use grade B real maple syrup, which is darker and more intense than grade A.

maple baked beans

dried navy beans or other small white beans, 2 cups (14 oz/440 g)

thick-cut bacon, 3 slices, diced

yellow onion, 1, chopped

salt

canola oil, 1 tbsp

cider vinegar, ¼ cup (2 fl oz/60 ml)

tomato paste, 2 tbsp

dry mustard, 1 tsp

cayenne pepper, ⅛ tsp

maple syrup, ⅓ cup (4 oz/125 g; see note)

MAKES 8–10 SERVINGS

Rinse the dried beans in a sieve under cold water. Pick over and remove any stones or broken beans. Set aside.

In the pressure cooker pot, sauté the bacon until it begins to render fat, then stir in the onion and cook until the bacon and onion are limp, about 3 minutes. Add the beans, 6 cups (48 fl oz/1.5 l) water, and a pinch of salt. Drizzle the oil over the liquid; do not stir. If using an electric pressure cooker, switch off the sauté function.

Lock the lid into place and cook on high pressure for 25 minutes. Let the steam release naturally (see page 17). When the pressure valve drops, remove the lid, tilting it away from your face to allow residual steam to escape. Stir together the vinegar, tomato paste, mustard, and cayenne; add the maple syrup. Pour the mixture into the pot, then simmer, uncovered and stirring frequently so the beans don't stick, until they are tender and the sauce is thickened, 12–15 minutes. Serve right away, or cool, cover, and refrigerate for up to 4 days (the beans will thicken as they stand). Reheat before serving.

Serve this dish with Pork Chile Verde (page 32), or as a vegetarian main dish made with vegetable broth. You can prepare beans ahead of time in the pressure cooker (see pages 98–99), but it takes less than half the usual time when you use canned beans.

brown rice & bean casserole

large yellow onion,
1, sliced

canola oil, 2 tbsp

butter, 1 tbsp, plus more
for greasing dish

cumin seeds, 1 tsp

salt

long-grain brown rice,
1½ cups (10½ oz/330 g)

**low-sodium vegetable or
chicken broth,** 3 cups
(24 fl oz/750 ml)

**cooked cannellini or
pinto beans (pages
98–99),** or 1 can
(15 oz/470 g), drained
and rinsed

sour cream, 1 cup
(8 oz/250 g)

freshly ground pepper

sharp Cheddar cheese,
⅔ cup grated (3 oz/90 g)

MAKES 4–6 SERVINGS

In the pressure cooker pot, sauté the onion in the oil and butter along with the cumin seeds and a pinch of salt until the onions are golden brown, 7–10 minutes. Add the rice and stir to coat with the onion mixture. Pour in the broth. If using an electric pressure cooker, switch off the sauté function.

Lock the lid into place and cook on high pressure for 18 minutes. Quick-release the steam (see page 17). When the pressure valve drops, remove the lid, tilting it away from your face to allow residual steam to escape. Stir the beans into the rice and let stand in the pot off the heat until the rice is cooled, about 10 minutes.

Meanwhile, preheat the oven to 375°F (190°C) and lightly butter the inside of a 7-by-9–inch (18-by-23–cm) baking dish.

Whisk the sour cream with a fork until smooth, then stir it into the rice and bean mixture. Season to taste with pepper. Spread the mixture in the baking dish and sprinkle the cheese over the top. Bake until crusty and bubbling at the edges, about 20 minutes. Serve hot.

PRESSURE COOK TIME

6
minutes

QUICK STEAM RELEASE

It's true: you can make a fantastic risotto in one quarter of the time in a pressure cooker. Vary this basic recipe with a pinch of saffron for risotto Milanese, a specialty of Milan, or stir in a cup of peas, beans, or other cooked vegetables at the end.

parmesan risotto

shallots, 2, or ½ yellow onion, finely chopped

butter, 1 tbsp

olive oil, 1 tbsp

arborio rice, 1½ cups (10½ oz/330 g)

saffron, pinch (optional)

dry white wine or vermouth, ½ cup (4 fl oz/125 ml)

low-sodium vegetable or chicken broth, 4 cups (32 fl oz/1 l)

parmesan cheese, ½ cup (2 oz/60 g) freshly grated, plus shavings for garnish

MAKES 4 SERVINGS

In the pressure cooker pot, sauté the shallots in the butter and oil until softened, about 2 minutes. Add the rice and saffron and cook, stirring, for 1 minute to toast slightly. Pour in the wine and stir until it evaporates. Pour in 3½ cups (28 fl oz/875 ml) of the broth. If using an electric pressure cooker, switch off the sauté function.

Lock the lid into place and cook on high pressure for 6 minutes. Quick-release the steam (see page 17). When the pressure valve drops, remove the lid, tilting it away from your face to allow residual steam to escape.

Stir the rice and taste for doneness: it should be al dente and the liquid should be soupy. If it is not done, stir in the remaining ½ cup (4 fl oz/125 ml) broth and cook over medium-high heat (or use the sauté function on an electric cooker) stirring, until the rice is cooked. Turn off the heat and stir in half of the parmesan. Serve, adding cheese shavings to each portion.

These all-purpose beans make for quick family meals, so make a big batch this way, instead of simmering them on the stove top for 2 hours. Serve them as a side dish alongside meat or poultry or rolled into a tortilla with rice for a quick burrito.

mexican-style pot beans

dried pinto beans,
1 lb (500 g)

thick-cut bacon,
2 slices, diced

canola oil, 2 tbsp

yellow onion, 1,
finely chopped

celery, 2 stalks, finely
chopped

dried oregano leaves,
1 tbsp

ground cumin, 2 tsp

sweet paprika, 2 tsp

cayenne pepper,
½ tsp

salt

beer, 1 bottle
(12 fl oz/375 ml; optional)

MAKES 10–12 SERVINGS

Rinse the beans in a sieve under cold water. Pick over and remove any stones or broken beans. Set aside.

In the pressure cooker pot, sauté the bacon in 1 tablespoon of the oil until lightly browned, but not crisp. Add the onion and celery and cook until softened, then stir in the oregano, cumin, paprika, cayenne, and a pinch of salt. Add the beans and 7 cups (56 fl oz/1.75 l) water. (Or for "drunken beans," substitute the beer for 1½ cups/12 fl oz/375 ml water.) Drizzle the remaining 1 tablespoon oil over the liquid; do not stir. If using an electric pressure cooker, switch off the sauté function.

Lock the lid into place and cook on high pressure for 30 minutes. Let the steam release naturally (see page 17). When the pressure valve drops, remove the lid, tilting it away from your face to allow residual steam to escape. Test a bean for doneness: it should be cooked through, but not mushy, and the sauce should be soupy, not thick. If the bean is still firm, lock the lid into place again and cook on high pressure for 5 minutes more; quick-release the steam (see page 17). Let the beans stand for 10 minutes to settle the flavors, then season to taste with salt.

To serve, ladle the beans into a large serving bowl, or cool, cover, and refrigerate with the liquid from the pot for up to 4 days (the beans will thicken as they stand). Reheat before serving.

Barley risotto usually takes 45 minutes of stirring, but here it's ready in less than twenty. Use whatever mushrooms you find in season in the market. When it isn't mushroom season, use cultivated white mushrooms, which are available year-round.

barley risotto with wild mushrooms

dried porcini, ½ oz
(15 g; about ½ cup)

boiling water, about
2 cups (16 fl oz/500 ml)

**mixed wild or regular
mushrooms,** 8 oz
(280 g), brushed clean

leek, 1

olive oil, 2 tbsp

dried thyme leaves,
½ tsp

pearl barley, 1½ cups
(9 oz/270 g)

**low-sodium chicken
broth,** 4 cups (32 fl oz/1 l)

parmesan cheese,
¾ cup freshly grated
(3 oz/90 g)

**salt and freshly
ground pepper**

**chopped fresh
flat-leaf parsley**
for garnish

MAKES 6 SERVINGS

Place the dried mushrooms in a large glass measuring cup. Add enough boiling water to measure 2 cups (16 fl oz/500 ml); set aside to soak until soft, about 30 minutes. Pour the porcini and soaking liquid through a sieve lined with a paper towel set over a bowl, reserving the liquid. Rinse the porcini of any grit, then chop. Set the porcini and strained liquid aside. Meanwhile, trim off the mushroom stem, and slice the mushrooms thinly.

Trim the root and most of the green tops off the leek. Cut it in half lengthwise, then thinly slice crosswise. Put the sliced leek in a bowl of cold water and swish well to rinse the leek of grit. Lift out the rinsed leek with a sieve or strainer and set aside. Discard the water.

In the pressure cooker pot, sauté the leek in the oil until softened, about 5 minutes. Add the sliced mushrooms and thyme and cook until the mushrooms soften, about 5 minutes. Rinse the barley in a sieve, then stir into the pot and add the chopped porcini, soaking liquid, and broth. If using an electric pressure cooker, switch off the sauté function.

Lock the lid into place and cook on high pressure for 18 minutes. Quick-release the steam (see page 17). When the pressure valve drops, remove the lid, tilting it away from your face to allow residual steam to escape. If a lot of liquid remains in the pot, cook on medium-high heat (or use the sauté function on an electric cooker), stirring, until the liquid is thickened slightly (risotto should be soupy; it will thicken as it stands), about 3 minutes. Stir in ½ cup (2 oz/60 g) of the parmesan and let stand for 5 minutes. Season to taste with salt and pepper and serve sprinkled with the remaining parmesan and chopped parsley.

PRESSURE COOK TIME
25 minutes
NATURAL STEAM RELEASE

With a touch of fresh ginger, sweet peppers, and nuts, this great holiday side dish is accomplished in half of the usual time. For a complete menu, you can let the salad stand while you prepare Turkey Breast with Cranberry-Ginger Relish (page 61).

confetti wild rice salad

wild rice, 1½ cups
(9 oz/280 g)

salt

olive oil, 6 tbsp
(3 fl oz/90 ml)

large red bell pepper,
1, diced

green onions, 2, thinly
sliced

**toasted sliced almonds
or chopped pecans,**
¾ cup (3 oz/90 g)

apple cider vinegar,
3 tbsp

soy sauce, 1½ tsp

fresh ginger, ½ tsp
grated

freshly ground pepper

MAKES 6 SERVINGS

Rinse the rice in a sieve under cold running water until the water runs clear; shake the sieve to get rid of excess water.

In the pressure cooker pot, combine the drained rice, 5 cups (40 fl oz/1.25 l) water, and ½ teaspoon salt; pour 1 tablespoon of the oil over the liquid, but do not stir.

Lock the lid into place and cook on high pressure for 25 minutes. Let the steam release naturally for 10 minutes, then quick-release the steam (see page 17). When the pressure valve drops, remove the lid, tilting it away from your face to allow residual steam to escape. Test the rice for doneness: it should be tender. If undercooked, lock the lid into place again and cook on high pressure for 5 minutes more; quick-release the steam. Drain the rice in a colander; rinse with cold water until the rice is cool to the touch.

In a large bowl, combine the rice, bell pepper, green onions, and nuts. In a small bowl, whisk together the vinegar, soy sauce, and ginger. Slowly whisk in the remaining 5 tablespoons (3 fl oz/80 ml) oil to make a dressing. Pour the dressing over the salad and mix well; season to taste with salt and pepper and serve.

meat

This recipe evolved from carbonnade—a classic Belgian beef stew, which is also delicious with meaty chicken thighs. Normally braised for 45 minutes, pressure cooking cuts the time by more than one-third. Serve the chicken and sauce over wide egg noodles.

beer-braised chicken thighs with onions

large bone-in chicken thighs, 6, about 6 oz (185 g) each, skin removed

salt

olive oil, 2 tbsp

butter, 1 tbsp

yellow onions, 2, thinly sliced

brown sugar, 1 tbsp

all-purpose flour, 1 tbsp

lager beer, 1 bottle (12 fl oz/375 ml)

coarse-grain mustard, 2 tbsp

tomato paste, 1 tbsp

bay leaf, 1

freshly ground pepper

cooked egg noodles for serving (optional)

MAKES 6 SERVINGS

Season the chicken lightly all over with salt. In the pressure cooker pot, brown the chicken in the oil in batches, turning with tongs as necessary; transfer each batch to a plate as it is browned. After removing the final batch, add the butter to the pot. When it melts, add the onions and sugar. Cook, stirring, until the onions are soft and golden, about 7 minutes, turning down the heat as necessary to keep them from scorching. Sprinkle the flour over the onions, then cook, stirring, for 1 minute. Pour in the beer and let it come to a boil. Stir in the mustard, tomato paste, and bay leaf. Return the chicken to the pot and turn with tongs to coat with the sauce. If using an electric pressure cooker, switch off the browning function.

Lock the lid into place and cook on high pressure for 11 minutes. Quick-release the steam (see page 17). When the pressure valve drops, remove the lid, tilting it away from your face to allow residual steam to escape. Remove the bay leaf and discard. Let the chicken stand for a few minutes to settle the flavors, then season to taste with salt and pepper. Serve right away over egg noodles, if desired.

Braised chicken usually requires browning, then cooking for 45 minutes. Amazingly, you don't need the skin for flavor or color when pressure cooking and it takes just a fraction of the time. Serve with rice or orzo to soak up the lemony sauce.

braised chicken in lemon-basil sauce

chicken, 1 whole, about 3½ lb (1.75 kg), cut into parts and skin removed

salt

butter, 3 tbsp

olive oil, 1 tbsp

shallots, 2 tbsp minced

dry white wine or dry vermouth, ⅓ cup (3 fl oz/80 ml)

low-sodium chicken broth, ½ cup (4 fl oz/125 ml)

fresh lemon zest, 1½ tsp grated

freshly squeezed lemon juice, ¼ cup (2 fl oz/60 ml)

paper-thin lemon slices, 6, seeds removed

fresh basil leaves, ⅓ cup (½ oz/15 g) chopped

MAKES 4–6 SERVINGS

Cut each chicken breast in half crosswise (or have the butcher do this) so that all 8 pieces are about the same size, which is important for even cooking. Season the chicken lightly all over with salt. In the pressure cooker pot, brown the chicken in 1 tablespoon of the butter and the oil in batches, turning with tongs as necessary; transfer each batch to a plate as it is browned. After removing the final batch, add the shallots to the pot and stir for 30 seconds. Pour in the wine and cook for 1 minute; add the broth, lemon zest, and juice. Put the lemon slices in the pot. Return the chicken to the pot, stacking the pieces so that the breasts are on top. If using an electric pressure cooker, switch off the browning function.

Lock the lid into place and cook on high pressure for 10 minutes. Quick-release the steam (see page 17). When the pressure valve drops, remove the lid, tilting it away from your face to allow residual steam to escape.

Using tongs, transfer the chicken to a serving platter and cover loosely with foil to keep warm. Strain the juices from the pot through a sieve into a frying pan; reserve the lemon slices. Boil on the stove top over high heat until the juices are reduced by one third, about 5 minutes. Cut the remaining 2 tablespoons butter into 4 pieces and add to the frying pan; swirl the pan until the butter is melted, then turn off the heat. Stir in the basil, season to taste with salt, and pour the sauce over the chicken. Garnish with the reserved lemon slices and serve right away.

This is the perfect weeknight recipe because it is comforting and quick—twice as fast in a pressure cooker as on the stove top. It can be doubled to feed a bigger crowd if you are entertaining. Ladle the stew over buttery egg noodles sprinkled with parsley.

beef stroganoff

beef bottom round,
1½ lb (750 g)

salt

canola oil, 3 tbsp

large shallot,
1, chopped

mushrooms,
½ lb (250 g), sliced

dry sherry, ¼ cup
(2 fl oz/60 ml)

low-sodium beef broth,
1½ cups (12 fl oz/375 ml)

tomato paste,
2 heaping tbsp

sour cream, ½ cup
(4 oz/125 g), at room
temperature

cooked egg noodles,
1 lb (500 g) for serving

sweet paprika
for garnish

MAKES 3–4 SERVINGS

Slice the beef into strips about 1 inch (2.5 cm) long and ½ inch (12 mm) wide. Season them lightly all over with salt. In the pressure cooker pot, brown the beef in 2 tablespoons of the oil in batches, turning with tongs as necessary; transfer each batch to a plate as it is cooked. After removing the last batch, add the shallot and the remaining 1 tablespoon oil and cook, stirring, until softened, about 2 minutes. Add the mushrooms and cook until they release most of their liquid and soften, about 5 minutes. Pour in the sherry and cook for 1 minute. Add the broth and tomato paste, stirring until blended. Return the beef to the pot. If using an electric pressure cooker, switch off the browning function.

Lock the lid into place and cook on high pressure for 18 minutes. Quick-release the steam (see page 17). When the pressure valve drops, remove the lid, tilting it away from your face to allow residual steam to escape. Let the stroganoff stand for about 5 minutes to settle the flavors. Whisk the sour cream with a fork until smooth, then stir it into the pot. Divide the egg noodles among warm shallow bowls, spoon the stroganoff over the top, sprinkle with paprika, and serve.

A turkey breast emerges moist and succulent from the pressure cooker in only 30 minutes versus 1½ hours in the oven. The key is to give it a good browning first so that the fat renders and the turkey takes on a caramelized surface.

turkey breast with cranberry-ginger relish

grated orange zest, from 1 navel orange

dried thyme leaves, ½ tsp

salt and freshly ground pepper

canola oil, 2 tbsp

boneless rolled and tied turkey breast, 1, about 3 lb (1.5 kg)

butter, 1 tbsp

low-sodium chicken broth, 1 cup (8 fl oz/250 ml)

cornstarch, 1½ tbsp

Cranberry-Ginger Relish (page 99), warmed for serving

MAKES 6 SERVINGS

Add the orange zest, thyme, ½ teaspoon salt, several grindings of pepper, and 1 tablespoon of the oil to a small bowl. Mix well, then scrape the mixture onto the turkey breast and rub it all over to coat every side.

In the pressure cooker pot, brown the turkey breast, starting with the fat-side down, in the remaining 1 tablespoon oil and the butter, turning with tongs, until brown all over. Once the turkey is browned, arrange it fat-side up in the pot. Pour the broth around the sides of the turkey. If using an electric pressure cooker, switch off the browning function.

Lock the lid into place and cook on high pressure for 30 minutes. Let the steam release naturally (see page 17). When the pressure valve drops, remove the lid, tilting it away from your face to allow residual steam to escape. Insert an instant-read thermometer into the center of the breast; it should be 160°F (71°C). If not, lock the lid into place and cook on high pressure for 5 more minutes, then let the steam release naturally again.

When the turkey is cooked, transfer it to a cutting board and snip the strings. Whisk the cornstarch and 1½ tablespoons cold water together in a small bowl, then stir the mixture into the liquid in the pot. Cook over medium heat (or use the sauté function), whisking, until thickened to make a gravy. Slice the turkey crosswise into slices about ½ inch (12 mm) thick. Serve with gravy and the warm cranberry relish.

Brisket generally takes about 3 hours to cook, but it comes out of the pressure cooker moist, tender, and full of flavor in just one-third of the time. Serve it on hamburger buns accompanied with the sauce and crunchy onions, pickles, and hot peppers.

barbecue-style brisket sandwiches

flat-cut beef brisket,
1, about 3½ lb (1.75 kg)

salt

ketchup, ½ cup
(4 oz/125 g)

brown sugar, ¼ cup
(2 oz/60 g) packed

Worcestershire sauce,
¼ cup (2 fl oz/60 ml)

apple cider vinegar,
¼ cup (2 fl oz/60 ml)

chili powder, 1 tbsp

sweet paprika, 1½ tsp

garlic, 1 clove, pressed

freshly ground pepper

yellow onion, 1, chopped

canola oil, 1 tbsp

soft hamburger buns, 8

**sliced red onions,
pickles, and pickled
hot peppers** for garnish
(optional)

MAKES 8 SERVINGS

Trim the meat of excess fat and pat dry with paper towels. Season lightly all over with salt; cut the meat crosswise in half to form 2 large pieces. In a bowl, whisk together the ketchup, sugar, Worcestershire sauce, vinegar, chili powder, paprika, garlic, and several grindings of pepper to make a sauce. Brush the brisket pieces all over with some of the sauce.

In the pressure cooker pot, sauté the onion in the oil until soft, about 3 minutes, then add ½ cup (4 fl oz/125 ml) water. Place 1 brisket piece on top of the onions and pour half of the remaining sauce over the meat; place the other piece of meat in the pot and pour the remaining sauce over it. If using an electric pressure cooker, switch off the sauté function.

Lock the lid into place and cook on high pressure for 60 minutes. Let the steam release naturally (see page 17). When the pressure valve drops, remove the lid, tilting it away from your face to allow residual steam to escape. Using tongs, lift out the meat and transfer it to a carving board. Let it rest for 5 minutes.

Meanwhile, with a large spoon or bulb baster, remove and discard as much fat as possible from the surface of the sauce. Thinly slice the meat across the grain and divide it among the bottom halves of the buns; spoon the sauce from the pot over the meat and garnish the sandwiches as desired before covering with the bun tops. Pass the remaining sauce in a small pitcher at the table to add to each portion as desired.

Traditionally, pot roast takes 2½ hours to oven-roast. Cut the roast into two pieces to pressure cook. It's easier to manage, and looks just as delicious when sliced and served. The sauce is thickened naturally with cooked vegetables.

classic pot roast with root vegetables

boneless chuck roast,
3½ lb (1.75 kg)

salt

canola oil, 1 tbsp

yellow onion, 1, sliced

carrots, 8, peeled and
cut into 1-inch (2.5-cm)
lengths

large parsnip, 1, peeled
and cut into 1-inch
(2.5-cm) lengths

dried thyme leaves,
1 tsp

dry white wine, ½ cup
(4 fl oz/125 ml)

low-sodium beef broth,
1½ cups (12 fl oz/375 ml)

tomato paste, 3 tbsp

bay leaf, 1

turnips, 1 lb (500 g),
peeled and cut into
2-inch (5 cm) lengths

**chopped fresh flat-leaf
parsley** for garnish

MAKES 6 SERVINGS

Pat the pot roast dry with paper towels and cut it in half to form 2 large pieces. Season lightly all over with salt. In the pressure cooker pot, brown 1 piece of meat in the oil, turning with tongs as necessary. Transfer to a plate and repeat with the other piece of meat. Add the onion to the pot and cook until softened, about 3 minutes. Add the carrots and parsnip to the pot and stir in the thyme. Pour in the wine and cook for 1 minute. Add the broth and tomato paste, stirring until the tomato paste dissolves. Stir in the bay leaf. Return the meat and any juices to the pot. If using an electric pressure cooker, switch off the browning function.

Lock the lid into place and cook on high pressure for 45 minutes. Let the steam release naturally (see page 17). When the pressure valve drops, remove the lid, tilting it away from your face to allow residual steam to escape. Transfer the meat to a plate and cover with foil to keep warm. Discard the bay leaf. Pour the sauce into a bowl and set it aside.

Pour 1 cup (8 fl oz/250 ml) water into the pressure cooker pot and add the turnips. Season lightly with salt. Lock the lid into place and cook on high pressure for 4 minutes. Quick-release the steam (see page 17). When the pressure valve drops, remove the lid, tilting it away from your face to allow residual steam to escape. Test the vegetables in the pot for doneness; they should be just tender. If necessary, continue to boil with the lid off until the desired doneness is reached. Slice the meat and arrange it on individual plates, then top with the vegetables. Remove the fat from the reserved sauce with a large spoon, then pour the sauce into a blender and purée. Spoon the puréed sauce over the meat and vegetables, sprinkle with the parsley, and serve.

Rich, thick Bolognese is one of the glories of the pressure cooker, making enough for a large batch of lasagne or to top 2 pounds of cooked pasta in one-fourth the usual time. Or use some now and store the rest for later when serving fewer people.

quick bolognese sauce

ground beef, 1 lb (500 g)

ground pork or veal, ½ lb (250 g)

olive oil, 3 tbsp

pancetta, 3 oz (90 g), finely diced

yellow onion, 1, chopped

carrots, 2, diced

celery, 1 stalk, diced

fresh flat-leaf parsley, ¼ cup (⅓ oz/10 g) chopped

garlic, 2 cloves, minced

salt and freshly ground pepper

dry red wine, ½ cup (4 fl oz/125 ml)

crushed tomatoes, 1 can (28 oz/875 g)

heavy cream, ½ cup (4 fl oz/125 ml; optional)

MAKES 6 SERVINGS

In the pressure cooker pot, sauté the beef and pork in 1 tablespoon of the oil, stirring to break up the meat, until browned. With a slotted spoon, remove the meat, then drain off the fat. Add the remaining 2 tablespoons oil to the pot with the pancetta, onion, carrots, and celery and cook, stirring, until the vegetables soften and the pancetta is lightly browned, about 4 minutes. Stir in the parsley, garlic, a pinch of salt, and several grindings of pepper and cook for 30 seconds. Pour in the wine and cook for 1 minute. Return the browned meat and any accumulated juices to the pot. Stir in the tomatoes and ½ cup (4 fl oz/125 ml) water. If using an electric pressure cooker, switch off the sauté function.

Lock the lid into place and cook on high pressure for 20 minutes. Quick-release the steam (see page 17). When the pressure valve drops, remove the lid, tilting it away from your face to allow residual steam to escape. Stir in the cream, if using. Let the sauce stand for 5 minutes to settle the flavors, then serve, or cool, cover, and refrigerate for up to 3 days. Heat through before serving.

Have the butcher "crack" each shank—that is, cut through the bone, but not entirely through the meat—so that it bends in the middle and is easier to brown. These shanks take just one-third of the time a traditional recipe requires.

greek-style lamb shanks with white beans

lamb shanks, 4, about 12 oz (375 g) each, cracked

salt and freshly ground pepper

olive oil, 2 tbsp

yellow onion, 1, sliced

garlic, 2 cloves, minced

dry white wine, ¾ cup (6 fl oz/180 ml)

low-sodium chicken broth, 4 cups (32 fl oz/1 l)

dried white beans, such as cannellini, 1¼ cups (9 oz/280 g)

fresh rosemary, 2 branches, about 4 inches (10 cm) long

tomato paste, 1 can (6 oz/185 g)

honey, 2 tbsp

ground cinnamon, ½ tsp

MAKES 4 SERVINGS

Season the lamb lightly all over with salt and pepper. In the pressure cooker pot, brown the shanks in the oil in batches, turning with tongs as necessary; transfer each batch to a plate as it is browned. After removing the final batch, add the onion to the pot and cook until softened, about 3 minutes. Add the garlic and stir for 30 seconds. Pour in the wine and cook for 1 minute. Stir in broth and beans, then add the rosemary branches. Return the shanks and any accumulated juices to the pot. If using an electric pressure cooker, switch off the browning function.

Lock the lid into place and cook on high pressure for 28 minutes. Let the steam release naturally (see page 17). When the pressure valve drops, remove the lid, tilting it away from your face to allow residual steam to escape. Test a shank for doneness by pulling on the meat with a fork; it should fall off the bone easily. If not, lock the lid into place again and cook on high pressure for 5–10 minutes. Let the steam release naturally again.

Using tongs, transfer the shanks to a plate; discard the rosemary branches. Cover the meat loosely with foil to keep warm. With a large spoon or bulb baster, remove as much fat as possible from the top of the sauce in the pot, then stir in the tomato paste, honey, and cinnamon. Boil the mixture over high heat (or use the browning function on an electric cooker) until the sauce is reduced and thickened and the beans are soft and creamy, stirring often, about 10 minutes. Divide the beans and sauce among shallow bowls and place a shank over each portion; serve right away.

PRESSURE COOK TIME

11

minutes

QUICK STEAM RELEASE

When pressure-cooked with an Asian-inspired sauce, these thighs don't have to be browned first: they come out lacquered with a dark glaze in one-third the usual time. For simple side dishes, serve steamed bok choy and brown rice alongside.

soy-glazed chicken thighs

low-sodium soy sauce, 1/3 cup (3 fl oz/80 ml)

dry sherry, 1/3 cup (3 fl oz/80 ml)

low-sodium chicken broth, 1/3 cup (3 fl oz/80 ml)

fresh ginger, 1 tsp grated

Dijon mustard, 1 tsp

large bone-in chicken thighs, 6, about 6 oz (185 g) each, skin removed

apricot jam, 1/4 cup (2½ oz/75 g)

cornstarch, 1 tbsp

MAKES 6 SERVINGS

In a nonreactive bowl, whisk together the soy sauce, sherry, broth, ginger, and mustard. Add the chicken, turn to coat with the mixture, and let the chicken marinate at room temperature for 30 minutes.

Transfer the chicken and marinade to the pressure cooker pot. Lock the lid into place and cook on high pressure for 11 minutes. Quick-release the steam (see page 17). When the pressure valve drops, remove the lid, tilting it away from your face to allow residual steam to escape.

Using tongs, transfer the chicken to a plate. Stir the jam into the sauce in the pot, then whisk until melted. Whisk the cornstarch with 1 tablespoon water in a small bowl until dissolved; stir into the sauce. Put the chicken back in the pot and turn with tongs to coat with sauce. Turn the heat under the pot to medium (or use the sauté function on an electric cooker) and simmer the chicken, with the lid on but not locked into place, until the sauce is thickened and glossy, 2–3 minutes. Serve right away.

While it's not traditional in Ireland, this is the dinner of choice on St. Patrick's Day in America. Usually requiring 3½ hours, it's much faster in the pressure cooker. An easy glaze and a short stint in the oven gives the meat extra flavor.

traditional corned beef & cabbage

corned beef brisket, 3½ lb (1.75 kg)

yellow onion, 1, cut into 2-inch (5-cm) chunks

celery, 1 stalk, cut into 2-inch (5-cm) lengths

garlic, 4 cloves, peeled

bay leaves, 2

lager beer, 1 bottle (12 fl oz/375 ml)

brown sugar, 3 tbsp packed

coarse-grain mustard, 2½ tbsp

apple cider vinegar, 1½ tsp

green cabbage, 1 head, cored and cut into 6 wedges

Yukon gold or red potatoes, 1½ lb (750 g), unpeeled and cut into 2-inch (5-cm) chunks

mini carrots, 1 lb (500 g)

MAKES 6 SERVINGS

Rinse the corned beef; if the meat has been cured with any whole spices, wipe those off as they can clog valves. In the pressure cooker pot, combine 2 cups (16 fl oz/500 ml) water, the onion, celery, garlic, and bay leaves. Rest the meat on top of the vegetables, placing it at an angle if necessary to fit. Pour the beer over the meat.

Lock the lid into place and cook on high pressure for 85 minutes. Quick-release the steam (see page 17). When the pressure valve drops, remove the lid, tilting it away from your face to allow residual steam to escape. Check to see if the meat is fork-tender; if not, lock the lid again and cook on high pressure for 10 minutes more, then quick-release the steam again.

During the last 20 minutes of cooking, preheat the oven to 425°F (220°C). In a small bowl, stir together the brown sugar, mustard, and vinegar. Line a baking sheet with aluminum foil.

Using tongs, lift the meat out of the pot and place it on the lined baking sheet, fat-side up. Blot the fat dry with paper towels. Spread the mustard mixture over the top of the meat. Put the meat in the oven and roast until the glaze is lightly caramelized, 10–15 minutes.

Meanwhile, remove and discard the cooked vegetables from the pot, but leave the broth. Add the cabbage to the pot, top with the potatoes, and then the carrots. Do not stir. Lock the lid into place and cook on high pressure for 5 minutes. Quick-release the steam (see page 17). When the pressure valve drops, remove the lid, tilting it away from your face to allow residual steam to escape. Remove the corned beef from the oven and carve into slices; arrange on a platter with the vegetables and serve.

Authentic Mexican-style pork tacos are made with *carnitas*, chunks of tender meat that have been braised for about 3 hours, then browned. Cooking them in the pressure cooker allows you to enjoy this traditional Mexican treat any day of the week.

pork tacos with cilantro slaw

for the pork

bone-in pork shoulder roast (pork butt or Boston butt), 2½ lb (1.25 kg)

salt

yellow onion, 1, quartered

chili powder, 1 tbsp

dried oregano leaves, 1 tbsp

garlic, 3 cloves, minced

for the tacos

flour tortillas, 12

Cilantro Slaw (page 99)

purchased salsa, 1 cup (8 fl oz/250 ml)

jack cheese, 1 cup (4 oz/125 g) shredded

Lime wedges for garnish (optional)

MAKES 6 SERVINGS

Cut the pork into 2 large chunks and pat dry with paper towels. Sprinkle with 1 teaspoon salt. In the pressure cooker pot, combine the onion, chili powder, oregano, garlic, and 2 cups (16 fl oz/500 ml) water. Add the pork pieces. Lock the lid into place and cook on high pressure for 50 minutes. Let the steam release naturally (see page 17). When the pressure valve drops, remove the lid, tilting it away from your face to allow residual steam to escape. Test the meat for doneness by prodding it with a fork; it should be easy to pull apart. If not, lock the lid into place again and cook on high pressure for 10 more minutes; quick-release the steam.

Transfer the meat to a cutting board and let it stand until cool enough to handle. While the meat is cooling, preheat the oven to 425°F (220°C). Line a baking sheet with foil.

Using 2 forks, pull the meat into shreds, discarding any bones and fat. Spread the shredded meat on the lined baking sheet and spoon enough juices from the pot over the meat to just moisten. Place the baking sheet in the oven and roast until the meat begins to sizzle and brown at the edges, about 10 minutes. Meanwhile, wrap the tortillas in foil and warm them in the oven.

To assemble the tacos, have diners put some shredded pork in a warm tortilla, top with a little of the slaw, and garnish with salsa, cheese, and lime wedges as desired.

Pork chops come out moist and flavorful in the pressure cooker, especially when quickly browned beforehand and topped with a vivid sherry vinegar–based sauce before serving. Serve alongside Scalloped Potatoes with Cheddar (page 82).

spanish-style pork chops with vinegar

smoked sweet paprika (*pimentón*), 1 tsp

salt and freshly ground pepper

bone-in pork chops, 4, about 6 oz (185 g) each

sherry vinegar, 2 tbsp

garlic, 1 clove, pressed

dried thyme leaves, ½ tsp

olive oil, 1 tbsp

low-sodium chicken broth, ⅔ cup (5 fl oz/160 ml)

MAKES 4 SERVINGS

In a small bowl, mix together the paprika, ¼ teaspoon salt, and several grindings of pepper. Rub the mixture over the pork chops. In another small bowl, whisk together the vinegar, garlic, and thyme.

In the pressure cooker pot, brown the chops in the oil, 2 at a time, turning with tongs to brown the fat along the edges; transfer each batch to a plate as it is browned. After removing the second batch, pour the vinegar mixture into the pot and cook for about 10 seconds, then add the broth. Return the chops to the pot, slightly overlapping them to fit. If using an electric pressure cooker, switch off the browning function.

Lock the lid into place and cook on high pressure for 2 minutes. Quick-release the steam (see page 17). When the pressure valve drops, remove the lid, tilting it away from your face to allow residual steam to escape. Serve the pork chops right away, with sauce spooned over each portion.

Saucy short ribs are a comfort food that usually requires 2 hours to cook, but here the time is reduced dramatically. Choose ribs that have been cut crosswise across the bones, usually referred to as Korean-style or Asian-style. Ask your butcher to cut them for you.

sticky asian-style short ribs

beef short ribs, 3½ lb (1.75 kg), cut Korean- or Asian-style

low-sodium soy sauce, ½ cup (4 fl oz/125 ml)

brown sugar, ⅓ cup packed (2½ oz/75 g)

tamarind concentrate, 1 tsp, or juice of 1 lime

garlic-chile sauce or *sambal,* ½ tsp, or ¼ tsp red pepper flakes and 2 minced garlic cloves

fresh ginger, 1 tbsp minced

hoisin sauce, ⅓ cup (3 fl oz/80 ml)

sliced green onions, green parts only, for garnish

steamed rice, for serving (optional)

MAKES 4 SERVINGS

Have the butcher cut the short ribs between the bones into about 6-inch (15-cm) lengths (or do this yourself) so they fit into the pot easily and cook evenly. In a bowl, stir together the soy sauce, brown sugar, tamarind, and garlic-chile sauce until smooth. Stir in the ginger. Add 1 cup (8 fl oz/250 ml) water and stir well to make a sauce.

Pour the sauce into the pressure cooker pot. Add the short ribs, turning them with tongs to coat with the sauce and arranging them tightly to fit in 1 layer. Lock the lid into place and cook on high pressure for 25 minutes. Let the steam release naturally (see page 17). When the pressure valve drops, remove the lid, tilting it away from your face to allow residual steam to escape. Using tongs, transfer the ribs to a bowl (do not worry if some meat separates from the bones). Meanwhile, preheat the oven to 400°F (200°C) and line a baking sheet with foil.

With a large spoon or bulb baster, remove and discard as much fat as possible from the top of the sauce in the pot. Boil the sauce in the pressure cooker over high heat (or use the browning function on an electric cooker), stirring often to prevent scorching, until reduced to about 1 cup (8 fl oz/250 ml). Stir in the hoisin sauce. Return the ribs to the pot, turning them with tongs to coat with sauce, then transfer them to the lined baking sheet. Bake in the oven until the sauce is glossy and baked on. Remove them and brush with the remaining sauce from the pot. Sprinkle with the sliced green onions and serve over steamed rice, if using.

PRESSURE COOK TIME
10 minutes
NATURAL STEAM RELEASE

There are probably as many recipes for stuffed cabbage as there are cooks who make it. This recipe is influenced by the style prepared in Hungary, in which it usually braises for 1 1/2 hours and sweet paprika flavors the filling.

hungarian-style cabbage rolls

green onions, 3

ground beef, 1 lb (500 g)

raw short-grain white rice, 1/4 cup (2 oz/60 g)

large eggs, 2, lightly beaten

sweet Hungarian paprika, 1 tbsp

garlic, 1 clove, pressed

salt and freshly ground pepper

green cabbage, 1 head, cored

yellow onion, 1, chopped

red bell pepper, 1, finely chopped

canola oil, 2 tbsp

chopped tomatoes, 1 can (28 oz/875 g)

sour cream, 1/2 cup (4 oz/125 g)

MAKES 6 SERVINGS

Set the green tops of the onions aside. Finely chop the white parts. In a large bowl, combine the ground beef, rice, the white part of the onions, the eggs, paprika, garlic, 1 teaspoon salt, and several grindings of pepper. Combine the mixture with your hands.

Bring a large pot of salted water to a boil, and place the whole cabbage, cored-side down, in the pot. Boil until the leaves soften, 3–4 minutes. Turn off the heat. Using tongs, pull off a cabbage leaf and place it on a cutting board. Using a 1/4-cup measure, scoop up some of the beef mixture and place it just inside the top of the cooked leaf, opposite the core end. Fold the leaf over the filling, fold in the sides, then carefully roll it up. Place each cabbage roll, folded-side down, on a plate and continue with the remaining beef mixture and leaves. Use a smaller amount of filling as the leaves get smaller, if necessary. Set the cabbage rolls aside.

In the pressure cooker pot, sauté the onion and bell pepper in the oil until just starting to brown, about 5 minutes. Stir in the tomatoes. If using an electric pressure cooker, switch off the sauté function. Place the cabbage rolls in the pot, snuggling them in to fit as necessary.

Lock the lid into place and cook on high pressure for 10 minutes. Let the steam release naturally (see page 17). When the pressure valve drops, remove the lid, tilting it away from your face to allow steam to escape.

Using tongs, transfer the cabbage rolls to individual plates. Let the sauce stand for about 5 minutes to cool, then stir in the sour cream. Thinly slice the reserved green onion tops. Spoon the sauce over the cabbage rolls and garnish with the green onion tops.

vegetables

PRESSURE COOK TIME
4 minutes
QUICK STEAM RELEASE

Ready in one-sixth the conventional time, this dish can be enjoyed two ways: as scalloped potatoes straight from the pot, or as au gratin potatoes when baked with bread crumbs. Buy potatoes that are all about the same size for uniform cooking.

scalloped potatoes with cheddar

large Yukon gold or medium white potatoes, 2 lb (1 kg)

low-sodium vegetable or chicken broth, 1 cup (8 fl oz/250 ml)

green onions, 2, green parts only, thinly sliced

salt

butter, 2 tbsp, plus more for greasing dish

all-purpose flour, 2 tbsp

half-and-half, 1 cup (8 fl oz/250 ml)

grated sharp Cheddar cheese, 1 cup (4 oz/125 g)

panko or other bread crumbs, 1/3 cup (1 1/2 oz/45 g; optional)

MAKES 6 SERVINGS

If making au gratin potatoes, preheat the oven to 375°F (190°C).

Slice the potatoes 1/4 inch (6 mm) thick, discarding the rounded ends. Pour the broth into the pressure cooker pot. Arrange the potatoes in even layers in the pot, being sure that the slices do not stick together. Scatter the green onions over the potatoes, then sprinkle generously with salt.

Lock the lid into place and cook on high pressure for 4 minutes (5 for white potatoes). Quick-release the steam (see page 17). When the pressure valve drops, remove the lid, tilting it away from your face to allow residual steam to escape. With a spatula or slotted spoon, transfer the potatoes to a warmed serving dish or, if making the au gratin potatoes, spoon them into a buttered 1 1/2-quart (1.5-l) baking dish. Strain the leftover liquid from the pot into a bowl.

In a medium saucepan, melt the butter over medium heat. Stir in the flour and cook for 1 minute, then pour in the half-and-half and whisk until thickened, about 3 minutes. Pour in the strained liquid from the pot and whisk until blended. Whisk in the cheese until smooth.

If making scalloped potatoes, pour the sauce over the potatoes in the serving dish. If making au gratin potatoes, pour the sauce over the potatoes in the buttered dish, sprinkle with the bread crumbs, and bake until bubbly and the bread crumbs are golden, about 12 minutes.

Mashed potatoes can take half an hour to prepare; but they're so easy to make in the pressure cooker, you'll want to serve them much more often. Offered with an assortment of additions or substitutions, you can vary the flavor every time you do.

creamy mashed potatoes

large russet potatoes,
3, about 2½ lb (1.25 kg),
peeled and cut into
2-inch (5-cm) chunks

salt

heavy cream, ½ cup
(4 fl oz/125 ml)

butter, 2 tbsp

MAKES 6 SERVINGS

In the pressure cooker pot, combine the potatoes, 6 cups (48 fl oz/1.5 l) water, and ½ teaspoon salt. Lock the lid into place and cook on high pressure for 5 minutes. Quick-release the steam (see page 17). When the pressure valve drops, remove the lid, tilting it away from your face to allow residual steam to escape.

Drain the potatoes in a colander and let them stand in the sink for 1 minute or so to evaporate any excess water. Put the cream and butter into the pressure cooker pot and warm over medium-high heat (or use the sauté function on an electric cooker); when the cream bubbles at the edges, pour the potatoes back into the pot. Turn off the heat. With a potato masher or heavy whisk, mash and stir the potatoes until smooth and thick. Season to taste with salt and serve right away.

variations

Horseradish Mashed Potatoes Stir in 2 tbsp cream-style horseradish.

Sour Cream Mashed Potatoes Melt the butter in the pot, but don't add the cream; return the potatoes to the pot and mash lightly, then beat in ½ cup (4 oz/125 g) room-temperature sour cream.

Buttermilk Mashed Potatoes Substitute ½ cup (4 fl oz/125 ml) buttermilk for the heavy cream.

Irish-Style Potatoes Thinly slice 3 green onions (both green and white parts) and sauté in the pot with the butter before adding the cream.

Cheddar Mashed Potatoes Stir in 1 cup (4 oz/125 g) grated sharp Cheddar cheese after mashing the potatoes.

This homey, nutritious side dish becomes quickly tender in the pressure cooker, rather than soggy during its traditional half-hour braise. It's great alongside pork chops (page 75) or served as a vegetarian entrée without the bacon.

sweet & sour red cabbage

red cabbage, 1 head, about 2 lb (1 kg)

thick-cut bacon, 3 slices, diced

canola oil, 1 tbsp

green onions, 4, green parts only, thinly sliced

low-sodium vegetable broth or water, 1/3 cup (3 fl oz/80 ml)

apple cider vinegar, 1/3 cup (3 fl oz/80 ml)

brown sugar, 1/3 cup packed (2 1/2 oz/75 g)

salt and freshly ground pepper

fresh goat cheese, 3 oz (90 g), crumbled

MAKES 4–6 SERVINGS

Cut the cabbage into 8 wedges and trim away the core. With a chef's knife, cut each wedge into thin strips.

In the pressure cooker pot, sauté the bacon in the oil until well browned and crisp, about 4 minutes. With a slotted spoon, transfer the bacon to a small plate. Add the onions to the drippings in the pot and cook, stirring, until softened, about 1 minute. Whisk in the broth, vinegar, sugar, 1/2 teaspoon salt, and several grindings of pepper. Stir in the cabbage. If using an electric pressure cooker, switch off the sauté function.

Lock the lid into place and cook on high pressure for 5 minutes. Quick-release the steam (see page 17). When the pressure valve drops, remove the lid, tilting it away from your face to allow residual steam to escape. Stir the cabbage well, then let it stand for about 5 minutes to settle the flavors. Divide the cabbage among plates and sprinkle each portion with the reserved bacon. Scatter the goat cheese over each portion and serve.

Winter squash takes far less time to cook to the right consistency for mashing when you use the pressure cooker. Pre-cut butternut squash can often be found in the produce section of the grocery store. Serve with turkey breast (page 61) if you like.

squash purée with brown butter & sage

butternut squash, 3 lb (1.5 kg) whole (or 2 lb/ 1 kg pre-cut cubes)

salt

butter, 3 tbsp

fresh sage leaves, 8

freshly ground pepper

MAKES 4–6 SERVINGS

If using a whole squash, peel it and cut it into 2-inch (5-cm) cubes, discarding the seeds and strings. In the pressure cooker pot, combine the squash cubes and 1 cup (8 fl oz/250 ml) water and season lightly with salt. Lock the lid into place and cook on high pressure for 8 minutes. Quick-release the steam (see page 17). When the pressure valve drops, remove the lid, tilting it away from your face to allow residual steam to escape.

While the squash is cooking, melt the butter in a small pan over medium-low heat. When the butter bubbles at the edges and is foamy, add the sage leaves to the pan. Reduce the heat to low and continue to cook, swirling the pan occasionally, until the butter solids are brown and the sage leaves are crisp, about 5 minutes. Using a slotted spoon, transfer the sage to a small plate. Set the sage butter aside.

Drain the squash in a colander. Put the drained squash in a large bowl and use a potato masher or the back of a large slotted spoon to mash it into a rough purée. Stir the sage butter into the mashed squash; season to taste with salt and pepper. Divide the squash among serving plates and garnish each serving with a fried sage leaf or two, crumbling the leaves over each portion, if desired.

You can make an impressive dish in minutes by using just the artichoke hearts. They'll be ready in one-sixth the usual cooking time. Pair them with Parmesan Risotto (page 44) for a vegetarian meal (cook the artichokes first).

braised artichoke hearts with peas & mint

lemon, 1

large artichokes, 4, about 10 oz (315 g) each

leek, 1, roots and green top removed

olive oil, 2 tbsp

dried thyme leaves, ¼ tsp

kosher salt

low-sodium vegetable broth or water, 1 cup (8 fl oz/250 ml)

fresh or frozen peas, 1 cup (5 oz/155 g), not thawed

butter, 1 tbsp

fresh mint leaves, 2 tbsp minced, plus whole leaves for garnish

MAKES 4 SERVINGS

Grate the zest from the lemon and set it aside. Fill a bowl with water and squeeze the juice from the lemon into it. Working with 1 artichoke at a time, snap off the dark green leaves until you reach the tender yellow inner leaves. With a small sharp knife, pare away any tough green leaf patches from the bottom of the artichoke, then trim the leaves 1 inch (2.5 cm) from the top. Cut each artichoke into quarters and, with a paring knife, trim away the fuzzy choke. Drop each quarter into the bowl of lemon water to prevent discoloring.

Slice the white part of the leek in half lengthwise, then thinly slice crosswise. Put the sliced leek in a bowl of cold water and swish to rinse it of grit. Lift out the leek with a sieve and set aside. Discard the water.

In the pressure cooker pot, sauté the leek in the oil until softened, about 3 minutes; stir in the thyme. With a slotted spoon, lift the artichokes out of the lemon water and add them to the pot; add a pinch of salt and pour in the broth. If using an electric pressure cooker, switch off the sauté function. Lock the lid into place and cook on high pressure for 4 minutes. Quick-release the steam (see page 17). When the pressure valve drops, remove the lid, tilting it away from your face to allow steam to escape.

With a slotted spoon, transfer the artichokes to a bowl; set aside. Add the peas and butter to the pot and bring to a boil over medium-high heat (or use the sauté function on an electric cooker). Cook, stirring, until the peas are just tender and the liquid in the pot has reduced, about 3 minutes. Stir in the minced mint and reserved lemon zest. Pour the peas, leeks, and juices over the artichokes and stir. Garnish with the whole mint leaves.

Beets take at least an hour when cooked on the stove top or roasted in the oven, but in the pressure cooker they are ready in a snap. Note that the size of the beet is crucial to how long it takes to cook, so select beets that are similar in size.

orange-glazed beets with fresh herbs

golden or red beets, 3,
about 6 oz (185 g) each

butter, 1 tbsp

freshly squeezed orange juice, ½ cup
(4 fl oz/125 ml)

honey, ½ tsp

salt

cider vinegar,
about 1 tsp

fresh flat-leaf parsley,
2 tbsp chopped

fresh mint leaves,
2 tbsp chopped

freshly ground pepper

MAKES 4 SERVINGS

Trim the tops from the beets, leaving about 1 inch (2.5 cm) of green stems attached; cut off any long roots. Scrub the beets well. Put the beets and 3 cups (24 fl oz/750 ml) water in the pressure cooker pot. Lock the lid into place and cook on high pressure for 20 minutes. Quick-release the steam (see page 17). When the pressure valve drops, remove the lid, tilting it away from your face to allow residual steam to escape.

Using tongs, transfer the beets to a plate, then rinse and wipe dry the inside of the pot. When the beets are cool enough to handle, use a paring knife to slip off their skins and trim away any remaining roots and stems. Slice each beet in half lengthwise, then cut each half into slices ¼ inch (6mm) thick.

Melt the butter in a wide nonstick frying pan over medium-high heat. Stir in the orange juice, honey, and a pinch of salt and bring to a boil. Add the sliced beets and shake the pan to coat the beets with liquid and spread them out; let the liquid boil, stirring occasionally, until the juices reduce and start to glaze the beets, 5–8 minutes. When almost all of the liquid has evaporated, transfer the beets to a serving platter. Sprinkle with the vinegar and the herbs. Taste and adjust the vinegar if necessary; season with salt and pepper. Serve warm or at room temperature.

This is the humblest of dishes and yet one of the most gratifying to prepare in the pressure cooker. What normally requires an hour of slow simmering comes out perfectly tender in a matter of minutes. Serve alongside pork chops (page 75), if you like.

southern-style braised greens with ham

mustard greens,
1 lb (500 g)

yellow onion, 1, chopped

ham steak, 6 oz (185 g),
finely diced

canola oil, 2 tbsp

dried thyme leaves,
½ tsp

red pepper flakes, pinch

**low-sodium chicken
broth,** 1½ cups
(12 fl oz/375 ml)

**cooked brown or white
rice,** 2 cups (10 oz/315 g)

hot pepper vinegar for
serving (optional)

MAKES 4 SERVINGS

Cut the tough stems from the mustard greens and discard; stack the leaves and cut them crosswise into 1-inch (2.5-cm) strips. Rinse the strips in a colander and shake to get rid of excess water. Set the greens aside.

In the pressure cooker pot, sauté the onion and ham in the oil until the onion softens, about 5 minutes. Stir in the thyme and red pepper flakes. Add the mustard greens and broth. If using an electric pressure cooker, switch off the sauté function.

Lock the lid into place and cook on high pressure for 6 minutes. Quick-release the steam (see page 17). When the pressure valve drops, remove the lid, tilting it away from your face to allow residual steam to escape. Stir the greens, then let them stand for a few minutes to settle the flavors. Ladle the greens, ham, and liquid over the rice in bowls and serve; pass the vinegar at the table for seasoning.

Little onions and peas in cream sauce are a holiday classic that normally takes twenty minutes, but comes together much more quickly in the pressure cooker. You can substitute frozen pearl onions, but fresh will give a far superior flavor.

creamed pearl onions with peas

white and purple pearl onions, 1 lb (500 g)

butter, 1 tbsp

low-sodium vegetable or chicken broth, 1 cup (8 fl oz/250 ml)

frozen peas, 1 lb (500 g), thawed

cornstarch, 2 tbsp

half-and-half, 2/3 cup (5 fl oz/160 ml)

freshly grated nutmeg, 1/4 tsp

salt

ground white pepper (optional)

MAKES 6 SERVINGS

Bring a saucepan of water to a rolling boil and drop in the onions; cook for 1 minute. Drain the onions, then transfer them to a bowl filled with ice water to stop the cooking. When the onions are cool enough to handle, use a small paring knife to cut off the tops and peel away the skins. Trim any long roots off the ends, but keep the root ends intact or the onions will come apart during cooking.

In the pressure cooker pot, melt the butter over medium-high heat (or use the sauté function), then add the onions and stir to coat. Pour in the broth. If using an electric pressure cooker, switch off the sauté function.

Lock the lid into place and cook on high pressure for 3 minutes. Quick-release the steam (see page 17). When the pressure valve drops, remove the lid, tilting it away from your face to allow residual steam to escape. Stir the peas into the onions. Stir the cornstarch into the half-and-half, then pour the mixture into the pot. Simmer, stirring, until the sauce is thickened and the peas are hot throughout, 3–4 minutes. Stir in the nutmeg and season to taste with salt and white pepper, if using. Serve right away.

Fennel is similar in texture to celery, with a subtle anise taste, and usually requires up to 30 minutes to tenderize. Near Nice, in southern France, it is often paired with tomatoes, garlic, and olives to make a hearty vegetable stew.

fennel niçoise

fennel bulbs, 3

garlic, 2 cloves, minced

olive oil, 2 tbsp

salt

dried thyme leaves,
½ tsp

dry white wine, ½ cup
(4 fl oz/125 ml)

plum tomatoes, 1 lb
(500 g), seeded and
chopped

unpitted Niçoise olives,
2 oz (60 g)

feta cheese, 4 oz
(125 g), crumbled

MAKES 4 SERVINGS

Cut the stems and fronds from the fennel bulbs, then cut the bulbs lengthwise into quarters. With a paring knife, trim away the cores. Cut the fennel crosswise into slices ½ inch (12 mm) thick.

In the pressure cooker pot, sauté the garlic in the oil until just fragrant, about 30 seconds. Add the fennel, ½ teaspoon salt, and the thyme. Sauté until the fennel starts to soften, 3–4 minutes. Pour in the wine and cook for 1 minute. Add ½ cup (4 fl oz/125 ml) water and the tomatoes, but do not stir. If using an electric pressure cooker, switch off the sauté function.

Lock the lid into place and cook on high pressure for 4 minutes. Quick-release the steam (see page 17). When the pressure valve drops, remove the lid, tilting it away from your face to allow residual steam to escape. Stir in the olives. With a slotted spoon, transfer the fennel, tomatoes, and olives to a 1½-quart (1.5-l) baking dish (discard the liquid in the pot).

Preheat a broiler. Sprinkle the cheese over the fennel mixture and broil until the cheese is browned and bubbly in spots. Serve right away.

basic recipes

boquet garni

fresh thyme sprigs, 6
fresh Italian parsley sprigs, 6
bay leaf, 1
celery, 4-inch (10-cm) piece
leek, 1, green part only, chopped

MAKES 1 BOQUET GARNI

Press the thyme, parsley, and bay leaf into the concave part of the celery; top with the green part of the leek and tie it all together with kitchen string. Use right away.

spicy croutons

soft white bread, 4 oz (125 g), cut into ½-inch (12-mm) cubes (about 2 cups)
sweet paprika, 1 tsp
salt
cayenne, ¼ tsp
ground cumin, ¼ tsp
butter, 2 tbsp

MAKES 2 CUPS (4 OZ/120 G)

Preheat the oven to 425°F (220°C). Put the bread cubes in a bowl. In a small bowl, stir together the paprika, ½ teaspoon salt, the cayenne, and cumin. Melt the butter and pour it over the bread cubes; toss well to coat. Add the spices and toss well again. Spread the cubes on a baking sheet and bake until crisp, about 10 minutes. Let cool, then use right away or store in an airtight container for up to 2 days.

cooked beans

dried beans, 1 cup (7 oz/220 g)
celery, 1 large stalk, broken in half
dried red chile, such as arbol, 1 (optional)
garlic, 2 cloves, peeled
salt, ¼ tsp
bay leaf, 1
canola oil, 1 tbsp

MAKES 2½ –3 CUPS (18–21 OZ/560–655 G) BEANS

Rinse the beans in a sieve under cold water. Pick over and remove any stones or broken beans. In the pressure cooker pot, combine the beans, 4 cups (32 fl oz/1 l) water, the celery, chile, if using, garlic, salt, and bay leaf. Drizzle the oil over the liquid; do not stir.

Lock the lid into place and cook on high pressure for 25 minutes. Let the steam release naturally. When the pressure valve drops, remove the lid, tilting away from your face to allow residual steam to escape. Test a bean for doneness: It should be cooked through, but not mushy. If it is still firm, lock the lid into place again and cook on high pressure for 5 more minutes; quick-release the steam.

Drain the beans, removing the celery, bay leaf, and chile (if used) with tongs. Set the beans aside. The beans can be cooled, covered, and refrigerated for up to 1 day. If using right away, bring to room temperature before use.

Note that cooking times may vary depending on the type of bean; see chart on page 10.

cilantro slaw

green cabbage, 4 cups (12 oz/360 g) shredded

cilantro leaves, 1 cup (1 oz/30 g), finely chopped

green onions, 2, finely chopped

mayonnaise, ¼ cup (2 fl oz/65 ml)

white wine vinegar, 3 tbsp

salt

MAKES 2½ CUPS (15 OZ/450 G)

Put the cabbage in a large bowl; add the cilantro and green onions. In a small bowl, whisk the mayonnaise and vinegar until smooth; pour over the cabbage and toss. Refrigerate, covered, for up to 2 hours. Season with salt and stir again before serving.

cranberry-ginger relish

fresh or frozen (thawed) cranberries, 3 cups (12 oz/375 g)

sugar, 1 cup (8 oz/250 g)

fresh ginger, 1-inch (2.5-cm) piece, peeled and chopped

seedless navel orange, 1

cornstarch, 1½ tbsp

MAKES 1½ CUPS (12 FL OZ/375 ML)

Place the cranberries, sugar, and ginger in a food processor fitted with the steel blade. Cut the orange into eighths and add it to the processor. Pulse until the mixture is very finely chopped. Transfer to a saucepan and bring to a boil over medium-high heat; reduce the heat, cover, and simmer for 10 minutes. Remove from the heat and let sit, partially covered, until ready to use.

tips for pressure cooking

- Read the instruction manual that comes with your model and always keep it handy

- Read through each recipe thoroughly before starting to cook

- Check the sealing ring or gasket every time you cook to make sure it is not dried, cracked, or stiff; clean it after every use

- Never fill the pot more than half full with food or two-thirds full with liquid (when making a soup, for instance) or the valves can become obstructed

- Each model requires a minimum amount of liquid; check the manual to be sure

- Drizzle oil over ingredients that foam, such as beans and grains, to keep them from clogging valves

- If using an electric pressure cooker, be sure to switch off the pre-cooking functions (such as brown or sauté) before switching over to the pressure-cook function

- If using a stove top model, have a digital timer set before you cook; do not turn it on until the correct pressure is reached

- Think of the amount of time it takes to build pressure as "preheating" your pot; it is not part of the cooking time

- Use your ears; if you hear the regulator valve hissing or spitting, it's telling you something needs adjusting

- When adapting your own recipes, it is better to err on the side of undercooking if you are not sure of the correct time; you can always close the pot and return it to pressure, or just simmer the food, until it is done

- Be sure to follow the instructions in each recipe for releasing pressure

- Do not place an electric pressure cooker underneath an overhead cabinet as the steam could damage the surface above when released

- Use caution when opening the pot: always tilt the lid away from your face since there is residual steam that can scald you

- Make notes on your recipe regarding cooking time, seasoning, etc., so that you can adjust accordingly the next time you prepare it

glossary

Anaheim Chiles A mild fresh green chile with a tough skin which must be removed before use, typically by oven-roasting or charring.

Apple Cider Vinegar A vinegar made from apples, noted for its distinctive fruit flavor. For the best results, buy real apple cider vinegar, not flavored distilled vinegar.

Arborio rice A Northern Italian variety of medium-grain rice. It's high surface-starch content makes Arborio the best choice for making risotto.

Artichokes A member of the thistle family, prized for their mild, nutty flavor. Artichokes are in season in early spring and late fall. Look for tightly closed olive-green leaves and healthy stems.

Barley An ancient grain, barley is essential to brewing Scotch whisky, as well as lending its delicious nutty flavor and chewy texture to stews and salads. Hulled, pearled barley is the most common and convenient form.

Bay Leaves Elongated gray-green leaves that impart a slightly sweet, citrusy, nutty flavor to sauces, soups, stews, and braises. Sold dried, bay leaves should be removed before serving.

Beans A pressure cooker dramatically cuts down cooking times for dried beans; times may vary for each batch, depending on how long they have been stored.

Cannellini These ivory-colored beans possess a creamy, fluffy texture when cooked.

Chickpeas Also known as garbanzo beans or ceci beans, these rich, nutty-flavored beans are beige in color, round in shape, and have a firm texture.

Lentils Small and flat, lentils come in many colors such as green, brown, and yellow. They are mild flavored, quick to cook, and extremely versatile.

Pinto Beans A pale brown bean with darker, pinkish streaks, which disappear during cooking.

Broth Any commercial stock made by simmering vegetables, chicken, beef, or fish in water is called a broth. Seek out low-sodium broths for more control in seasoning.

Canola Oil This neutral-tasting oil is pressed from rapeseed, a relative of the mustard plant. High in monounsaturated fat, it is good for general cooking.

New Mexico Chiles Large red or green fresh New Mexico chiles are moderate to hot in flavor; they are available fresh or dried.

Farro This ancient strain of wheat is also sometimes known as emmer, frequently used in Italian cooking. A wholesome grain, farro's texture is quite chewy, with a nutty flavor.

Fennel A bulb vegetable with slim stems, relative to celery, with a faint licorice flavor and a crisp texture. The feathery fronds can be used as a seasoning or garnish.

Feta A white, crumbly sheep or cow's milk cheese that is cured in brine, imparting a salty, tangy flavor. Feta is a traditional Greek cheese, though now commonly made abroad.

Green onions Also known as scallions or spring onions. Green onions are the immature shoots of the bulb onion, with a narrow white base, and long, flat green leaves.

Harissa A fiery North African spice paste of chiles, spices, garlic, and olive oil, which doubles as both seasoning and condiment. Sold in well-stocked grocery stores and Middle Eastern markets.

Hoisin Sauce A thick, brown, salty-sweet sauce, hoisin is used both as an ingredient and as a condiment in Chinese cooking. It is made with soybeans, garlic, vinegar, chiles, and other flavorful spices.

Hominy Soft, white, puffed-up kernels of corn, which are the result of drying, soaking in lime or lye, and boiling for several hours. Sold as whole kernels or coarsely cracked, it is delicious in soups and stews, especially in Mexican cooking.

Leek Resembling a giant green onion, with its bright white stalk and its long, overlapping green leaves, the leek is the mildest member of the onion family, and is integral to classic French cuisine.

Maple Syrup Maple syrup is made by boiling down the sap of the sugar maple tree to an amber colored syrup. Darker grade B or cooking maple syrup have the most robust flavor.

Mushrooms, Dried Porcini A dried wild mushroom with intense aroma and flavor; in cooking, just a small dose yields full, woodsy flavor.

Olives, Niçoise Small black olives named for the city of Nice in France's Provence region. Niçoise olives are not very fleshy, but they have a rich, meaty, relatively mellow olive flavor.

Orzo The Italian word for "barley." This pasta shape resembles large, flat grains of rice. It is particularly well suited for use in soup and salad preparations.

Panko Japanese dried breadcrumbs, which are exceptionally delicate and deliver light, crisp texture to fried foods. Look for bags or boxes in specialty food stores and Asian markets.

Parmesan An ivory-colored cow's milk cheese with a distinctive, salty flavor. A wonderful grating cheese.

Parsnip An ivory-colored root vegetable, resembling its relative the carrot, with a sweet flavor and a tough, starchy texture that softens with cooking. Excellent roasted, steamed, boiled, or baked.

Potatoes, Yukon Gold A medium-starch potato with thin skins and yellow flesh, Yukon gold potatoes have a sweet, butter flavor. They are a good all-purpose potato.

Sherry, dry A fortified wine from Southern Spain, sherry is made from the Palomino Fino grape. Dry sherry is mild in sweetness and is often used in cooking.

Sherry Vinegar True sherry vinegar from Spain, labeled *vinagre de Jerez*, has a slightly sweet, nutty taste, a result of aging in oak.

Soy Sauce A mixture of soybeans, wheat, and water is fermented to make this savory, salty Asian sauce. Chinese dark soy sauce is thicker and sweeter, due to the addition of molasses.

Spices When possible, buy whole seeds and toast and grind them yourself for superior flavor.

Chili Powder A commercial spice blend which combines dried chiles, cumin, oregano, garlic, cloves, and coriander.

Cumin A seed from the parsley family with sharp, strong flavor, common to Latin American, Indian, and Moroccan cooking. Available ground or whole.

Coriander The dried ripe fruit of fresh coriander, or cilantro. The seed adds an exotic flavor to both savory and sweet foods, including stews and baked goods.

Paprika, Sweet A Spanish specialty made from red chiles that have been smoked and then ground, yielding earthy, smoky flavor and deep red color.

Cayenne Pepper A very hot ground red pepper made from dried cayenne and other chiles.

Madras Curry Powder A complex mixture of ground chiles, spices, seeds and herbs. Indian home cooks blend their own. Madras has more heat than standard curry powder.

menu ideas

lunchtime

moroccan-style tomato-
rice soup (page 21)

green salad

crusty bread

———

summer barbecue

barbecue-style brisket
sandwiches (page 62)

cilantro slaw
(page 99)

potato chips

watermelon slices

———

weeknight dinner

braised chicken in
lemon-basil sauce (page 57)
with cooked orzo pasta

mixed green salad

holiday supper

turkey breast with cranberry-
ginger relish (page 61)

confetti wild rice salad
(page 51)

creamy mashed potatoes
(page 84)

dinner rolls

———

cold weather comfort

texas-style chili
(page 31)

southern-style braised
greens with ham (page 92)

cornbread

———

mexican fiesta

pork chile verde (page 32)

mexican-style pot beans
(page 47)

corn tortillas

guacamole

salsa

mediterranean light

curried cauliflower soup
with spicy croutons
(page 26)

chickpeas with lemon,
oregano & olives (page 41)

fennel niçoise (page 96)

———

italian supper

cooked rigatoni pasta
topped with quick
bolgonese sauce
(page 66)

braised artichoke hearts
with peas & mint
(page 88)

———

asian night

soy-glazed chicken thighs
(page 69)

steamed rice

sweet & sour red cabbage
(page 85)

index

weldon**owen**

415 Jackson Street, Suite 200, San Francisco, CA 94111
Telephone: 415 291 0100 Fax: 415 291 8841
www.weldonowen.com

Weldon Owen is a division of

BONNIER

WELDON OWEN INC.

CEO and President Terry Newell
VP, Sales and Marketing Amy Kaneko
Director of Finance Mark Perrigo

VP and Publisher Hannah Rahill
Executive Editor Jennifer Newens
Editor Donita Boles
Editorial Assistant Becky Duffett

Associate Creative Director Emma Boys
Art Directors Alexandra Zeigler and Kara Church
Senior Designer Ashley Lima
Junior Designer Anna Grace

Production Director Chris Hemesath
Production Manager Michelle Duggan
Color Manager Teri Bell

Photographer Sheri Giblin
Food Stylist Karen Shinto
Prop Stylist Christine Wolheim

THE PRESSURE COOKER COOKBOOK

Conceived and produced by Weldon Owen Inc.
Copyright © 2010 Weldon Owen Inc.

All rights reserved, including the right of reproduction
in whole or in part in any form.

Color separations by Embassy Graphics in Canada
Printed and bound by 1010 Printing, Ltd. in China
First printed in 2010
10 9 8 7 6 5 4

Library of Congress Cataloging-in-Publication
data is available.

ISBN-13: 978-1-74089-983-3
ISBN-10: 1-74089-983-0

ACKNOWLEDGMENTS

Weldon Owen wishes to thank the following people for their generous support in producing this book:
Linda Bouchard, Ken Della Penta, Shay Harrington, Cathy Lee, Fanny Pan, and Ann Rolke.